Echo

Aris Austin

Echo

Copyright © Aris Austin 2018

Published by Austin Joseph

Denver, CO

ISBN 978-1983656101

This book is for all my wonderful friends who are alive because of open rescue. It's also for the wonderful humans who risked their safety and freedom to save them.

Most of all though, this book is for the animals who never made it out. I promise we'll keep fighting for you until we make it stop.

Chapter 1

His name was EK-230. He knew it wasn't much of a name for a Beagle, or anyone else for that matter. It was the only one he had, though. EK-230 was the name they assigned him when they took him from his mother. It was the name they wrote down whenever they made a note about him. The name they'd tattooed inside his left ear.

The humans were responsible for all of it. Humans, with their long, white coats and latex gloves. And their needles. *So many needles.* EK-230 hated needles. He wanted to hate the humans too. It would be easier to stop trusting them if he hated them, but he couldn't find it in himself to do that.

Besides, not all humans were bad. There was the kindly man who came each evening to fill their food and mop the floors. He even cleaned out the pans under the dogs' cages, which was a relief after living above a heap of excrement all day.

There was also Caitlyn, the intern. She was nice most of the time, and a hint of citrus always clung to her tightly bound ponytail—a welcome change from the stench of the cage. Sometimes, she called EK-230 "Eee-Kay." He liked that.

It was easier to remember, and it made him feel a little less like a piece of lab equipment.

Caitlyn entered the room just then, and EK wagged his tail. Caitlyn's arrival usually meant a walk. Walks were fun, and being excited was okay as long as it was just Caitlyn. If she had come with Jansson, the assistant researcher, the walk would have been a trap. *Those* walks always ended in the lab. Jansson was nowhere in sight though, so EK happily allowed Caitlyn to loop a leash around his neck and lead him into the hallway. He loved the time out of the cage, even if a "walk" actually just meant a short march around the hall. The route never changed: down to the front doors, around a few corners, past the stairs, and then back to the cage. EK had always dreamed that someday, Caitlyn would extend the walk by taking him through the front doors. That she'd let him blink in the sun and sniff at the air, or even chase a few birds back into the bushes. That would be the best day of his life.

It was only ever a dream, though. EK lingered by the front door when they reached it, but it didn't take long for Caitlyn to drag him away. She was always in a hurry.

EK, on the other hand, wasn't exactly eager for the next part of the walk. He didn't like having to pass the door to the lab. He pressed against the wall as soon as they rounded the corner, straining against his leash to get as far from the door as possible. He knew Caitlyn didn't like pulling, but he couldn't risk being noticed by a researcher. *They* were the dangerous kind of human.

"It's *okay*, EK. It's Sunday. Dr. Ross isn't even here!"

EK relaxed a little. Flatiron Life Labs was a safer place without Dr. Ross, although that wasn't saying much.

Plenty could still happen on the days he wasn't around. Jansson knew how to take weights. She knew how to strap the dogs into their harnesses and fit masks on their faces. She knew how to make them breathe caustic air from the masks, and how to answer their ragged coughs with assurances that they were doing a "*very* important job." At least there wouldn't be needles, though. Only Dr. Ross handled the needles, though EK had yet to figure out why.

"Up you go!" said Caitlyn.

EK returned to reality just in time to watch Caitlyn lift him back into the cage. *Strange.* He couldn't even remember walking around the other corners or past the stairs. It must have happened at some point though, since they were back. Sometimes, EK didn't think his mind worked quite right. All the time in a cage made it hard to focus when there were actually things worth focusing on.

EK watched Caitlyn lead the dog from the adjacent cage into the hall. *His sister.* Caitlyn called her HK. They'd been close once, but they hadn't spent much time together since the breeders took them from their mom. Thanks to the opaque dividers between their cages, EK only got to see his siblings in the lab, and the lab wasn't exactly a good place for reunions. Sometimes, it was infuriating that he could be close enough to smell them and not actually be *with* them.

EK wondered if HK looked out the front doors with the same longing he did. *Caitlyn had to take them outside someday*, he thought. *Just for a few moments.* He'd seen the way she looked through the doors. She wanted to go out, too. It hadn't happened yet, but he could dream.

Dreaming was one of the only good ways to pass time in the cage. It was too small for walking or running, and all EK could do with his siblings was listen to their movements. He could hear the shuffling of their paws, or their eating, or sometimes even their peeing. There was never any talking, though. Eliminating all talking was the first thing the researchers had done when EK arrived at the lab. The man he'd come to know as Dr. Ross had placed a needle in his forelimb. He'd fallen asleep only moments later, and he woke up in a cage with a sharp pain in his throat. Barking had been impossible ever since. Any time he tried, all that came out was a harsh rasping sound.

EK sighed and settled down to the floor of his cage. *No sense in staying awake after the daily walk was over.*

The hard steel grate that made up the floor wasn't exactly comfortable, but lying down was better than letting the bars dig into his paws. And anyway, sleeping usually made the discomfort go away. Sleep was the one escape EK-230 still had. Sometimes, he thought that if he could fall asleep forever, he would.

He didn't sleep for long, and his only dream was a rather frightening one about climbing the stairs in the hallway. No matter how long he climbed, he couldn't ever seem to reach the top, and the bottom somehow disappeared from view every time he tried to turn around. There was no way out, and it didn't seem like the ordeal would ever end. Fast or slow, it didn't matter. The top never came. He was actually grateful when the pan sliding out from beneath his cage woke him.

EK-230 blinked at the man emptying the pan into the trash. He was one of the only humans EK didn't mind seeing, so it was a shame his visits were always so short. He only stayed as long as it took to finish the cleaning and feeding, and sometimes he disappeared for days at a time. Someone else came on the days he was gone, but she never acknowledged EK or his siblings. EK was sure there was some kind of pattern to it, but he hadn't been able to figure one out yet.

The man slid the pan back under EK's cage and smiled. He smiled quite a lot, but his eyes always retained a deep sadness, and that sadness grew even stronger on the days the dogs had been to the lab. EK wondered if the man actually felt sorry for them. *Could humans feel emotions like empathy?* EK supposed it was possible.

EK watched the man slide fresh bowls of food and water into his cage. His hand was dark and covered in sunspots, which made EK wonder if perhaps he was more likely than Caitlyn to take the dogs outside. He'd never even taken any of them for a walk though, which made the idea seem unlikely.

The man caught EK staring and quickly reached up to scratch his ears. EK immediately flinched away, and a pained expression fell across the man's face.

"Perdóname," he said. "I have no want to frighten you."

The man spoke very little English, but that didn't bother EK. He understood Spanish about as well as English, which wasn't well. No one took the time to teach him many words.

"Lo siento," the man sighed. He turned away and began cleaning the next cage.

EK understood *those* words, and began feeling sorry in return. He didn't like making the sad-eyed man even sadder.

Flinching was a reflex, but the man had never hurt any of them. He hadn't even taken them to the lab, like Caitlyn sometimes did. And he seemed upset when the dogs were in pain. *Maybe there's no need to be scared of him,* EK thought. *He could be a friend.*

The man finished his cleaning and headed for the door, but he glanced over his shoulder before leaving.

"Lo siento," he said again. He looked at each of the dogs. "I will fix this."

With that, the man disappeared into the hallway and locked the door behind him. He claimed he would "fix this" nearly every day, but EK didn't know what that meant. It seemed to him that the way to fix it would be to let them all free outside.

No matter. He didn't expect much fixing to come from any human. They didn't seem dependable enough for that. Every time he heard the man's promise though, EK-230 couldn't help but feel a glimmer of hope. *Maybe things could get better. He could dream, couldn't he?*

Chapter 2

There were four of them: EK, his sisters HK and FK, and his brother, GK. All weighed, all lined up on the countertop, all strapped into their harnesses. EK-230 could already tell it was going to be a bad day.

He offered his siblings one last glance before Jansson fastened down his breathing mask. The mask itself didn't obscure his vision, but it wouldn't be long before the tears did, and he wanted to look at his family while he still could.

GK's pad was bleeding. *Had he torn the scab off again?* It had been weeks since he first hurt his paw, but he was always so busy chewing on it that it never had a chance to heal. EK sighed. He wanted to comfort his brother, but he knew there was no use in trying while the harness had him trapped in place. He *hated* that the only time he got to see his siblings was in the lab.

The breathing mask slipped, and Jansson cursed before starting the tightening process over. EK briefly considered biting her hand, but he couldn't bring himself to do it. He'd always *known* biting was an option, and that it would probably keep the mask off for at least a few more moments. He hadn't ever tried, though. None of them had.

Jansson cinched down the mask—too tight—and patted EK's head. "Good boy. You'll do a good job for us today, right?"

EK lowered his gaze to the countertop. He didn't like Jansson.

Dr. Ross spoke then, his voice barely audible from his spot across the room. He always spoke in low, soft tones, which inevitably caused Jansson to leave the dogs and stand closer to him.

"Concentration twenty-two hundred parts-per-million. Opening flow at 9:51 A.M., rate of 1.2 liters per minute."

EK did his best to ignore the hum of the pump switching on, focused instead on the sounds of Jansson punching numbers into her tablet, or of HK struggling in her harness. The harnesses kept them from leaving or even sitting down, but EK didn't blame his sister for trying. The pump was scary. It meant bad air was coming.

EK-230 couldn't pinpoint exactly when he first detected the bad air. It had no taste, and the smell always crept up on him rather than coming all at once. He could feel it, though. The icy way it swirled down his throat, splashing against his lungs before retreating in an exhale. The cold always came first. Then his nose would tingle, and an itch would inevitably form in his throat. When the study first began, that was all the bad air had done. It had actually been somewhat tolerable back then. EK suspected they were mixing in more and more of whatever substance tainted the air each time, though. And that meant things were about to get worse.

"9:54 A.M., increasing flow rate to 1.4 liters per minute."

EK resisted the urge to cough as the itch in his throat turned to a burning sensation. Coughing only helped to dislodge solid things like food, and air couldn't be dislodged. If he started coughing, he wouldn't be able to stop until the humans took his mask off. He'd learned that the hard way. The trick to getting through it was slow, shallow breaths in the bottom of his throat. That, and the knowledge that it would all be over soon.

Tears formed in EK's eyes, but he managed to swallow another cough. HK wasn't so lucky. She only let out a gentle cough at first, but quickly turned to thrashing and sputtering as each fit grew more violent than the last. *Poor HK,* EK thought. *Coughing already.*

It took several moments, but HK somehow managed to calm herself down and return to normal breathing. EK knew that wouldn't last for long, though. His sister had been coughing every time recently, and she had suffered for it.

"9:57 A.M., flow rate to 1.6 liters per minute"

Why would the humans make it worse? To see how much they could take? To see how tough they were? If that was true, EK didn't want to be tough anymore. He wanted to be soft and safe, in a soft and safe place.

"10:00 A.M., flow rate to 1.8 liters per minute."

HK's coughing started up again, much worse than before. EK winced. Coughing without vocal cords was harsh and grating, like a chair being dragged across the floor in short, jerking bursts. He wondered if it was possible to die from coughing so hard with no voice to help.

Someone on the other side of HK burst into their own coughing fit. *GK?* Between HK's fits and the tears in his own eyes, it was impossible for EK to tell. Either way, it scared him. HK was usually the only one to cough. *Why were the humans making it worse? What did they want?*

Somehow, HK's cough grew even more intense. A hollow choking sound came from deep in her throat, and her whole body went stiff as a half-digested sludge forced its way out of her stomach. It hit the breathing mask with a wet slopping sound, and then she was silent.

A fear worse than anything EK had ever felt stabbed through his heart. *Was his sister dead? What had the humans done to her? Was anyone safe, or would the rest of them die next?*

HK let out a weak cough, and EK slumped against his harness. *She was okay.* He wanted to go to her, wanted to rip the mask away with his teeth and clean the mess from her face. He was still strapped into the harness, though. The best he could do was listen to Dr. Ross's droning voice, only inches from the counter and somehow still audible over the dogs' coughing.

"10:07 A.M., test subject HK-230 has vomited into its mask."

HK got a single gasp of clean air as Dr. Ross scooped the sludge from her mask. Then the strap tightened back down, and a fresh round of coughing followed. EK winced again.

"Removing debris from subject's mask so breathing can continue," Dr. Ross said. "Sample does not appear to contain blood at first glance. Further analysis is necessary to be certain."

A little huff of air forced its way out of EK's throat. *That was almost a cough. He needed to be more careful.* He couldn't do anything for HK just then, and if he started coughing, it wouldn't be long before he ended up like her. *Just focus,* he told himself. He leaned forward, letting the harness take his weight. *In. Out.* Every breath burned all the way down and all the way up again. EK retreated deep inside himself, to a place where the pain didn't feel so real. *Just focus,* he thought. *In. Out. In. Out. In.*

***

The humans ended up stopping the bad air only shortly after HK threw up, but she continued coughing for a long time. Even at the end of the day, EK could still hear his sister wheezing in her cage. He couldn't imagine what she was going through. *His* throat was still burning, and he hadn't even been coughing all day. He had tried to wash the burning out of his throat with water, but it was still there even after he had licked his bowl dry. The humans were *definitely* making it worse.

The man with the sad eyes entered the room then, signaling the end of the day. He smiled at the dogs for a moment, but his face fell when he realized what had happened.

"Dios mío," he muttered. He dropped his cleaning supplies and rushed to fill HK's water, then quickly attended to the rest of the dogs' bowls. EK greedily lapped at the water, plunging his whole face into the bowl before the man even set it down. It didn't help much, but at least it was something.

EK wished he knew the man's name. He was so kind, but since none of the other humans ever spoke to him, there was no way to know what he was called.

"I will fix this. Soon," he said. Then he added to himself, "May the Lord perdón us. What we do here is truly the work of the devil."

He reached out, and this time, EK stepped forward to meet him. The man could just barely reach EK's ears through the bars, but being pet actually felt—*good. Had he ever been pet by a human before? He certainly couldn't remember being pet.* His tail whipped back and forth, beating against the side of the cage.

EK-230 licked at the man's fingers stared into his eyes. They looked absolutely heartbroken at the dogs' pain. Not for the first time, EK wondered how this man could care so much when other humans seemed so callous. *And what did he mean by saying he would fix this?*

"I will fix this," the man said again. And when he left without locking the little room's door, EK-230 decided maybe—*maybe*—he could trust him.

Chapter 3

EK-230 couldn't sleep. He'd been trying since the man with sad eyes left, but it had been nearly half the night, and still no sleep came. Something always managed to wake him just as he was beginning to drift off. A renewed burning in his throat that wouldn't leave until he stood up for a drink. The occasional rasping cough from his sister. And always, *always* the knot in his stomach that tightened every time he thought of the lab.

He tried to keep himself occupied with the various sounds of nighttime. There weren't many noises at night, but the few that existed were much more pleasant than the daytime sounds. No footsteps coming down the hall to bring him to the lab. No squeaking cart carrying lethal instruments to some unseen room. At night, there was only the breathing of his siblings and the gentle cycling of the air conditioning. And so EK-230 found himself quite shocked when he heard a voice— a *human voice*—float into the hallway.

"Sentinel, I'm inside. Our guy left the first door unlocked just like he promised. Can you still hear me in here?"

EK stood up, suddenly alert. *A brand new human voice! And in the middle of the night?* He didn't know if he should be more excited or terrified.

A second voice—*someone called Sentinel?*—crackled through a spotty phone connection. "Yeah, I hear you An—"

The owner of the first voice interrupted him by loudly clearing her throat.

"—I hear you, *Ghost*," Sentinel continued in an exasperated tone. "Tell me why we're using codenames again? You said you needed help with an *open* rescue, not a bad spy movie."

"It's—some of the shit you see in these places," said the human named Ghost. "It's nice to find a way to lighten it up a little. Being Ghost while I'm here helps me sleep at night. I get to leave her at the door, and she's tougher than me. Besides, this works much better if nothing is "open" until we want it to be."

She paused. "Do you have the floorplans ready?"

"Yeah," Sentinel crackled. "If our guy picked out the server closet correctly, it'll be on the second floor. Take a right from the main doors and follow the hallway to a staircase. Room A-208 should be unlocked. The closet is inside. Once I'm in their system, I should be able to tell pretty quickly whether I can access the security cameras.

"Okay. You might have to repeat that once I'm up there. Thank you again for agreeing to help. I know it seems over the top, but I don't want things to end up like that university last year. They kept us from getting anyone out once they caught on…"

Ghost's voice faded as she climbed the stairs. It was ages before it finally returned.

"It worked?"

"Yeah," Sentinel replied. "There aren't as many cameras as I hoped, though. I can only monitor the halls, so if you want footage from the lab, we'll have to hide a camera in there. The lab should be room A-144. That one might be locked, though."

Ghost was quiet for a moment. "The only camera I have besides my phone is the one I'm wearing. It's pretty small, so I could hide it. Where are the dogs? I want to go there first."

"A-102."

The door handle jiggled only a few heartbeats later. A woman slipped into the room and gently shut the door behind her.

"Got it," she said.

EK-230 flattened himself against the floor of his cage. He didn't think the human had spotted him yet, and he wanted to keep it that way until he knew her intentions. The light from her headlamp was blinding in the otherwise dark room, but EK didn't look away. As frightened as he was, he couldn't help but feel a sense of fascination with this turn of events. *No one had ever shown up in the middle of the night before.*

Ghost's face was difficult to see until she took off the headlamp and set it on a nearby shelf. As soon as she stepped into the light, EK scanned her for signs of danger. Her face was round, despite the bun of mousy-brown hair pulled back so tight that it seemed to tug at the corners of her cheeks. Her skin was the color of the dry sandy swirls that occasionally crept by the front door on windy days. She seemed to be...EK had never been good with human ages. She was older than

Caitlyn, but certainly younger than any of the other humans at Flatiron Life Labs.

The equipment she carried was minimal. A white biosecurity suit covered her body from her ankles to her to neck, decorated only by a small camera clipped to the collar. A barely-noticeable pair of earbuds were nestled in her ears, presumably connected to some unseen device tucked deep inside the suit. She didn't *seem* dangerous. But then again, there weren't exactly *any* humans who seemed dangerous at first glance. They were tricky like that.

As Ghost moved closer, EK noticed a slight limp in her walk—a hesitation in her knee that forced her hip to compensate by swinging out to the side. Still, she moved with a strength and certainty that made her seem to glide across the floor.

"Hi sweetie." Ghost stopped in front of EK's cage. "How long have you been watching me?"

EK-230's only answer was a wide-eyed stare. *He'd been caught.*

"Don't worry," she said. "I'm not here to hurt you. Your water's almost gone though! Let me fix that."

Ghost's fingers worked at the cage's latch, opening the door just enough to slip EK's water bowl through the gap. EK managed to resist the urge to shrink back. He didn't move any closer either, though. *Courage was one thing, but there was no sense in taking needless risks.*

"Wouldn't want you to be thirsty!" said Ghost. Her voice had an almost cheerful quality to it, despite the tension on her face. Whenever she spoke, EK found himself thinking of the chirping birds who lived in the bushes outside. *This human really did seem safe. He didn't think she wanted to hurt him.*

Ghost reached back into the cage and set EK's bowl inside, accidentally splashing a little water over the edge. Her eyes met EK's then, and she tentatively reached toward him.

"Is it okay if I pet you?" Her hand hovered only a short distance from EK's face, waiting for a response.

Despite his better judgement, EK stood and sniffed at Ghost's hand. *Why was he still so ready to trust?* Nearly every human who received his trust abused it, but he couldn't help it. He *wanted* their warmth and love, just like he wanted it from his siblings.

Ghost's fingers were cold, but they scratched EK's head just fine, and he decided temperature didn't really matter when it came to being pet. What mattered was the touch—the affection it communicated.

Two friendly humans in one day, he thought. He wondered how many friendly humans there could be. He wondered if maybe, there were some who *wouldn't* abuse his trust, and if Jansson and Dr. Ross might become friendly if he just gave them a chance. *What if that was it? What if he just hadn't given them enough of a chance yet? What if things could still change?* It was something to hope for, at least.

"See how affectionate he is?" Ghost said to the camera. "Researchers like using Beagles because they're trusting and easy to work with, even when they're being hurt. That might be the worst part of this. They trust us, and this is what we give them in return."

She stopped scratching EK's head then—far too soon, in his opinion—and moved on to refill HK's water.

"Your eyes are all red and puffy, sweetie. Did the people here do that to you?"

Ghost tugged at her suit, angling the attached camera toward HK's face. "Even in the dim light, you can see how thin she is. The muscles in her neck and shoulders aren't nearly as rounded as they should be. And it's hard to tell without knowing her age, but she seems smaller than the average Beagle. Part of that comes from being in a cage all the time, but you can see that she's also been throwing up a lot."

Throwing up? Only in the lab. But EK smelled it as soon as Ghost pointed her camera at the floor of HK's cage. It was there, alright. HK had thrown up *much* more than just that one time in the lab. *Why hadn't he heard, or even smelled it before? And why did life in the cage make it so hard to think?*

"I'm sorry you're sick, baby," said Ghost. "I'll know more about what they're doing after I visit the lab. Then we'll be a little closer to getting you out, okay?"

EK lost sight of Ghost after she moved on to meet FK and GK. Their cages were behind his, and the solid plastic dividers were impossible to see through. Except for the brief appearances Ghost made to refill his siblings' water bowls, EK could only hear her.

"Look at his paw," she said to the camera. "He's been chewing on it all day. And the floor of this cage probably isn't helping. See how it digs in every time he takes a step?

"That pacing he's doing is called a stereotypy. It's a behavior a lot of captive animals take on—a sort of last-ditch effort to keep themselves sane. I've seen it in pigs, dogs, even elephants.

"I wish I had some ointment for your paw, buddy. I can't imagine having to stand on that mesh all day. I'd wrap it up, but then they'll know someone was here. I'll make sure to at least bring something to clean it out next time, though. Try not to bite it, okay?"

EK pondered the way Ghost talked to them. She didn't come off as having a sense of superiority like the other humans did. She talked to them like equals, and he *liked* that. It made him feel like he deserved to be treated well. Like he deserved more than this, and she knew it.

"Aw, are you too sleepy to meet new people right now? That's okay. I know you've probably been having a rough time. Rest well, sweetie. Good night."

Ghost crossed back into EK's line of sight. She panned the room with her camera for a few moments, then straightened and said to seemingly no one, "So I just realized the camera I'm wearing can only record a few hours of film before it dies. It probably only has about an hour of charge left, and I want to make sure it catches what's actually happening in that lab. If I hide it in the lab, can you power it on remotely?"

Sentinel's voice crackled through Ghost's headphones. "Is it connected to the internet at all?"

"No…I don't think so."

"I can't do anything with it, then. But I could with your phone. Just know that if they find it, you aren't going to get it back. And all they have to do is figure out how to unlock it and they'll be able to find you."

Ghost thought for a moment. "If they found it, could you keep them from getting in?"

"I have a program that bricks the phone after three failed attempts at unlocking it. That's the best we can do tonight, though. The other option is to go home and come back later."

Ghost was silent for a while. Then she took a deep breath. "Let's just do that program. I don't know how many more times I'll be able to get in here, and I don't want to risk an unnecessary trip."

"Okay," said Sentinel. "Head to the lab. I'm going to send you an email with two attachments. Download and save them to your phone so I can remote in. I'll tell you what to do from there."

"Got it."

Ghost turned to the dogs. "Bye puppies. I'll be back for you someday, I promise." Then she slipped into the hallway, taking the light with her.

Chapter 4

The days tended to run together at Flatiron Life Labs. By EK-230's count, it had been seven, or maybe eight or nine days since the night he met Ghost. He had started to wonder whether she was actually coming back, but he still couldn't stop thinking about her. *She'd been so kind.* EK wanted to meet more humans like her. If there *were* more humans like her. EK thought he saw a glimmer of that kindness in the humans from the lab sometimes, but it was horribly unpredictable. And some of them even seemed capable of acting kind and cruel in the same heartbeat.

As if on cue, the door swung open and Caitlyn stepped into the room. EK was glad to see her for a moment, but his heart sank as soon as Jansson appeared behind her. *No. Not again.* His throat had only just started feeling better. *It was too soon. It couldn't already be time to go back.* Jansson never showed up for plain old walks, though. EK swallowed hard.

As usual, Jansson tried to pet EK when she opened his cage, and as usual, he ducked out of the way. A faintly hurt expression crossed her face, which gave him a moment of pause. *What if Jansson really did want to be friends, like*

Ghost? He hadn't ever given her the chance. What if that was all she needed?

EK shook himself, then stepped forward and nuzzled Jansson's hand. *He had to show he wanted to be friends first. Then maybe she would have the courage to do the same.*

The look on Jansson's face turned to a smile. "Looks like someone's feeling cuddly today."

Caitlyn glanced up from the floor, where she was tightening HK's leash. "Who, EK? That's weird. He's never cuddly. *This* is the cuddly one, once she gets to know you."

She patted HK and stood. "I guess he just takes even longer to get used to people than she does."

Jansson laughed. "Five months? He'd be the shyest dog I ever met."

She lifted EK out of his cage and set him on the floor. "You shouldn't name them, you know. The live portion of the study is going to be over soon, and getting attached just sets you up for a bad couple of days when we move onto dissection and analysis."

EK thought he saw Caitlyn wince, but he wasn't sure why. "I'm not naming them. Just dropping the last part of their ID numbers off. EK-230 is kind of a mouthful."

Jansson gave a noncommittal nod and moved on to leashing up FK. FK had always been the toughest of them, but even *she* smelled of fear that morning. They all knew where they were going, and they all knew it was going to be worse. EK wasn't the only one who could recognize patterns, after all.

Unnerving as FK's fear was, EK couldn't help but hang onto a tiny bit of hope. *Maybe Jansson would be nice to them in the lab.* He *had* let her pet him, after all. *Maybe she would just weigh them and let them go. No harnesses, no masks, and no bad air.* He clung to that idea as Caitlyn opened the door and led the entourage outside. *It was a new day, and new days could always be different.*

The hallway lighting cast the same harsh glow as usual, and the world waiting through the front doors was rainy and gray. *That was no good.* EK hated wasting his daily glimpse outside on bad weather. There were no birds when it rained, and the clouds only made him feel gloomy. It wasn't even worth the effort to fight for a pause at the doors in that kind of weather. That should have made the humans happy, but they were too busy whispering about someone named Mr. McMachen to notice. They didn't even pay attention when GK stopped to use the bathroom. In fact, the only thing that managed to get their attention was the gentle slap of fresh poop against linoleum.

"Oh, *seriously* dude?" Caitlyn's voice carried an unusually frightening amount of force. All of the dogs—especially GK—ducked away from her angry gaze. The leashes kept them from going far, but it was worth a try.

Jansson raised her eyebrows at Caitlyn. "They aren't toilet trained."

"I know," Caitlyn said, pulling out a plastic bag. "But that's the third time this week. It feels like he's doing it on purpose."

On purpose? EK mused over his brother's genius. *Pooping on the walk was smart. That would keep it out of the tray beneath his cage, and he wouldn't have to smell it all day.*

It was such a smart idea that EK decided to try it out right there. Following his brother's lead, he squatted down to relieve himself. The humans caught on much more quickly that time, and the only thing louder than Jansson's laughter was Caitlyn's shrill command.

"EK STOP!"

EK was so startled that he actually *did* try to stop, but it was already too late, and the best he could do was give Caitlyn a wide-eyed stare as the poop fell to the floor. Caitlyn didn't find that nearly as amusing as Jansson did. She glared at EK the entire time it took to clean up the mess, and even shot him an angry glance as she tossed it in a nearby trash can.

"After we drop them off, make sure to come by and disinfect those spots." Jansson motioned to the traces of debris left on the floor. "I don't know when Mr. McMachen is coming, but he can't be seeing that."

Caitlyn nodded and shot the dogs another withering look. Her anger set EK on edge, but to GK's credit, pooping in the hall *was* much better than going in the cage. He also couldn't help but notice how relaxed Jansson seemed about it all. *Could it actually have been that simple? All it took to make her friendly was a little affection?* EK could hardly believe it, but it gave him hope. *Maybe there wouldn't be any bad air in the lab. Maybe Jansson would protect them.*

A young man pushing a cart nearly ran the dogs over as they rounded another corner. He apologized profusely to Jansson and Caitlyn, who apologized in return and turned to walk around the cart. Before EK could follow the humans though, something on top of the cart piqued his curiosity. He knew the humans would be cross, but he couldn't *not* get a closer look at whatever was up there. And maybe if he was *just* quick enough, they wouldn't notice. He did a little half-leap, gripping the top of the cart with his paws. His nose only barely reached the edge, so he had to crane his neck to see—

EK froze. Four tiny creatures had been splayed out on their backs and cut open from throat to tail. The objects he had first seen from the floor were neatly folded labels, attached to pins that stuck out of each creature's body at varying angles. An image of Dr. Ross holding a needle flashed across EK's mind, and he shuddered. *Could Dr. Ross do that to him? Slice him open and fill him with needles?*

The man pushing the cart swatted at EK's face only a heartbeat before Jansson yanked on the leash. Several human voices issued commands, but EK-230 was too stunned to listen. His head spun almost as much from being hit as from what he'd seen. *Pins and needles. Death.*

Jansson swam into view only inches from EK's face. "No! Mice are *not* for eating! Bad dog!"

EK wanted to protest, but humans rarely understood what he tried to tell them. Instead, he bowed his head and followed Jansson down the hall without so much as another glance at the cart. His heart pounded out a worried beat in his chest. *Had he just ruined his friendship with Jansson? Could he still earn it back?* He resolved to be a very good dog for the rest of the day. He *had* to convince Jansson not to make him breathe the bad air. To not let Dr. Ross cut him open and fill him with needles like the mice.

EK, FK, and Jansson entered the lab right on the heels of Caitlyn and the other dogs. Dr. Ross was already waiting inside, accompanied by a middle-aged man with graying blonde hair. The blonde man's presence must have disturbed Jansson, because EK heard her stutter for the first time in his life.

"S—oh, um, sorry we're a little late. There were a couple of small incidents in the hall. It's all taken care of, though."

"That's alright," Dr. Ross said, emotionless as usual. "Mr. McMachen, this is my research assistant Jennifer, and this year's intern, Caitlyn."

Jansson shifted the leashes to her left hand and reached out to Mr. McMachen. "It's nice to meet you."

McMachen smiled warmly. "You as well, Jennifer. And it's nice to meet you, Caitlyn. An intern…so are you a student at the university?"

"Yes," Caitlyn said. "I'm studying biology, and hopefully I'll go onto a PhD program in a couple of years."

"Well," said McMachen. "It's a good school. I went there. Keep up the good work, young lady."

"Mr. McMachen has asked to observe our work today," said Dr. Ross. "I already told him how much we appreciate a busy company executive taking the time to learn the science behind everything, so let's not keep him waiting."

Caitlyn handed HK and GK's leashes to Dr. Ross and quietly excused herself. Jansson and Dr. Ross began their work with even less conversation than usual, but McMachen seemed willing to fill in the gaps.

"Dr. Ross tells me you're nearing the end of the trials. I'm so glad to hear it. What's *your* opinion on the research, Jennifer?"

Jansson lifted EK onto the scale. "My opinion doesn't really matter. The data should speak—"

"Oh no, don't tell me that," McMachen interrupted. "Dr. Ross already tried. Of *course* your opinion matters. That's the whole reason we hire you. Data itself is meaningless. What we need is someone qualified to interpret it."

EK wished his trembling legs would hold still. Scales made him nervous, because the humans always took weights before and after the bad air. *If he was extra good for Jansson though, maybe she wouldn't punish him this time...*

"Alright..." Jansson seemed hesitant. "My opinion on what part?"

"You know," McMachen made a sweeping motion with his hands. "All of it."

"Well, we were up to 2,200ppm for 30 minutes last week." The scale chirped, and Jansson lifted EK off. "And they're still alive. Only moderate weight loss in all four subjects since the beginning of the trial, though it's starting to pick up in a couple of them."

McMachen's face grew stern. "And is 2,200ppm a lot?"

Dr. Ross's voice drifted across the room so quietly, EK didn't know how the humans could even hear him.

"The aerosolized concentration of the dose in a standard load was in single digits when we first measured it. We've been increasing it every week. None of them seemed even a little sick until a few weeks ago."

McMachen clapped his hands together and said something in a cheery voice, but EK didn't care to listen. *He had to figure out how to get out of breathing the bad air. What did the humans want?*

Jansson lifted him back onto the counter by the scale, snapping him out of his thoughts. She had apparently already weighed his other siblings, because Dr. Ross was on his way back across the room with a fistful of vials. *Be a good boy,* EK told himself. *Bad air is worse than needles. Show them there's nothing to punish.*

The first time EK had his blood drawn, he had knocked glass equipment all over the floor. Humans didn't like it when he broke things, so maybe being perfectly still would make them proud. Then they wouldn't *need* to make him feel sick, because good dogs didn't need to be punished. EK steeled himself as the needle went in, focusing his attention on the ever-present sound of McMachen's voice.

"…This is the biggest investment we've ever made, but the payoff should be huge. Most laundry detergents— including our current line—have been using the same old cocktail of active ingredients for years. Dichlorotetrahexane uses less water than anything on the market though, and tests showed colors lasting 40% longer. And since it only requires such low concentrations, we can undercut everyone else. Imagine disrupting the laundry detergent market, of all things! Shares of Oasis are going to hit an all-time high."

EK let out a sigh of relief as Dr. Ross removed the needle. *Done.*

"And you two can get in on those profits, you know. We like to reward talent at Oasis. I'm sure we could set up a lab and procure whatever test subjects you need. Work directly for our R&D department instead of this—" he motioned at the ceiling "—middleman, and we'll be sure to pay you more. I'm sure you would especially benefit, Jennifer. We adopted an equal pay for women initiative the same year I started the company. It's something we're known for."

EK thought he saw the corners of Jansson's mouth turn upward, but she lifted him off the counter before he could get a better look.

"There'd be formalities, and we'd want to see you do a good job of finishing up with the right results here, of course," McMachen added. "But you'd both have my personal recommendation."

Jansson carried EK to the testing bench and strapped him into a harness. She turned away, suddenly very interested in Mr. McMachen, and EK's gaze fell. *What had he done wrong? He'd been such a good boy. He had hoped being extra good would mean no more punishments...*

Jansson returned with HK and quickly strapped her into the second harness. *Maybe he had been naïve, but he couldn't help it. There was good in humans. He'd seen it in Ghost, and in the man with the sad eyes. Why didn't Jansson have it?*

Jansson and Ross worked faster than usual, and it wasn't long before all four dogs had been strapped in and fitted with masks. EK stared at the humans from his spot on the counter, sick with anticipation. He knew this pattern. They were nearly ready to turn on the bad air. *And then what would happen? How much worse would it be?*

Jansson nodded at Dr. Ross, who said, "twenty-four hundred parts per million, flow rate 1.2 liters per minute."

Then the pump kicked on, and EK-230's heart sank.

***

Breathe, EK told himself.

Dr. Ross had already increased the flow rate twice, and EK's lungs burned like acid. His eyes had filled with so many tears that he couldn't even make out the countertop beneath him. The best he could do was keep his head bowed, listening for anything that could draw his attention away from the bad air. The *tap-tap-tap* of Jansson's fingers on her tablet. The rhythmic clicking of the pump. HK's violent coughing. Dr. Ross's droning voice.

"It only looks bad today," said Dr. Ross, "because they're inhaling concentrations fourteen times higher than what you'd get if you dropped a whole box of detergent into steaming hot water. Of course, we'll know much more after postmortem testing—we're hoping to move to that within the next couple of weeks."

"Mm." There was a hint of concern in McMachen's voice, but then he seemed to steel himself. "So the product will pass your tests then?"

Dr. Ross gave a noncommittal response that was nearly lost when GK joined HK's coughing. EK felt a deep stabbing in his own throat, but he forced the cough back down. *Breathe.*

McMachen's voice grew uncharacteristically cold. "Have you been taking data down throughout the study?"

"…yes."

"And does the data suggest DCTH will pass? We can't just be doing this to these dogs for nothing, you know. I happen to have a dog at home, and I don't want any needless suffering."

A twinge of frustration entered Ross's voice. "...Yes. Normal concentrations are much lower than the threshold for reactions, and even very high concentrations seem to be safe in the short term. But it's unwise to make any conclusions before—"

"Well there you go!" McMachen said, suddenly cheery again. "That's all I was asking for. The board will be happy to hear it! I'll inform them that the final results will be available at the end of next week."

Dr. Ross cleared his throat. "Flow rate to 1.8 liters per minute."

A small cough escaped EK's lungs, followed by several larger ones. *No!* He strained against his harness, as if the pressure alone could force the coughing to stop. *Breathe,* he thought. *No coughing. Just fight it. Just breathe.*

Somehow, it worked.

"It is...unlikely that we'll have results by then, sir. We need high enough concentrations to elicit a significant reaction from all four dogs. Then we'll need to index that concentration with government standards—"

HK's breakfast forced its way out of her stomach, slopping against her mask so loudly that Dr. Ross lost his train of thought. EK winced. *That had to have hurt.* He hoped it would take Jansson a long time to clean HK's mask so she could get at least a few clean breaths in. Pathetic as it was, hoping was the most he could do for his sister right then.

A violent coughing fit suddenly tore through EK's throat. He tried to regain control the way he had before, but it was too much. The air was too strong. He coughed by reflex, not by choice, and there was no stopping it.

He thought he heard FK start coughing shortly after that, which was *very* bad news. FK had always taken the bad air silently and stoically. If *she* couldn't hold out, there wasn't much hope for the rest of them.

Please, EK pleaded in his thoughts. *Please make it stop. Jansson. McMachen. Ghost. Someone help us.*

By some miracle, the pump powered down only moments later. EK slumped against his harness, gasping for air between coughing fits. *It's over,* he told himself. *Breathe now. It's over. It's over.*

"What concentration do you need to elicit a *significant reaction?*" McMachen's voice echoed over the dogs' coughing, but whatever response Dr. Ross gave was much too quiet to hear.

"Turn it up, then."

EK lifted his teary gaze, blinking in disbelief.

"Uh…well, we're actually done for today, sir." Dr. Ross said. "We should maintain as much consistency as we can throughout the experiment."

McMachen didn't take his eyes off the dogs. "We're on a schedule here, Dr. Ross. The board wants the product out by the end of the year. We're going to need to keep going until we get some results."

For a moment, EK wondered how the warmth could have disappeared from McMachen's eyes so quickly. The sound of the pump starting up again cut off his thoughts.

"Resuming at previous flow rate of 1.8 liters per minute," said Dr. Ross. "Concentration increased to twenty-six hundred parts per million."

Somewhere down the counter, Jansson tapped the numbers into her tablet. HK coughed, as did GK. EK didn't take his eyes off McMachen. *Please, don't.* A hint of concern flashed across the man's eyes, but it wasn't enough to move him.

If the bad air had been like acid before, this new concentration was fire. *Liquid, noxious fire.* EK choked on his own attempt to swallow, his throat closing down into a hole no larger than one of Dr. Ross's needles.

Please, he begged, tears welling up in his eyes. But McMachen just stood there, arms crossed and eyes cold. The world spun violently, and EK's stomach spun with it. He collapsed against his harness, desperately straining for air. And he coughed. He was long past trying to fight it. It was the only way he could get a little air, but even with that, it felt like he was suffocating. *Drowning.* Drowning in a lab far from the ocean, with three expressionless humans watching him sink.

Chapter 5

EK hadn't been *really* sick for a while, but the room still spun when he closed his eyes. The sad-eyed man had cleaned up the dogs' vomit at the end of the day, but EK had thrown up more after that. The smell of it made him want to throw up all over again. Or it would have, if he had anything left *to* throw up.

Only heartbeats after Mr. McMachen demanded another concentration increase, all four dogs had started throwing up. EK had done it *twice* before even leaving the lab. Each time, Jansson had removed his mask to wipe most of the mess into a beaker, but then she just stuck the mask right back on. EK had been certain he was going to die. He could hardly even remember having his blood drawn after the masks came off, and he'd lost count of how many times he and his siblings threw up after being returned to the cages.

He had tried standing to get a little farther from the rancid mess in his pan, but that didn't last long. He was just *so tired.* Lying on the cage's floor was all he could bear to do. His throat *still* burned, and the metallic taste of blood mingled with traces of vomit in his mouth.

Mr. McMachen was *not* a good human. He only made things worse. And for all EK's efforts, Jansson had done absolutely nothing to help him. Sure, there had been the usual petting and exclamations of "you are such a good boy. You are doing *such* important work!" after she returned him to his cage, but what good were words when all she ever did was hurt him?

EK should have been happy when he heard the gentle patter of footsteps in the hallway. *Ghost.* Who else could it have been? Even *she* hadn't been there to help though, and EK wondered if his trust in her had been misplaced.

Another set of footsteps joined Ghost's, and EK wondered who they might belong to. *The human on the phone, maybe? Sentinel. That was his name.*

The footsteps faded with the gentle shutting of a door, but returned only moments later. Muffled voices echoed down the hall with them.

"Looks like no one found it," said a deep, unfamiliar voice. *Not Sentinel. Someone new?*

"Yeah," said Ghost. "Hopefully it actually caught what they were doing in there before it died."

"Should we plug it in? There's an outlet over here."

Low-quality audio spilled into the hallway, interrupted each time someone skipped to new parts of the footage. EK bristled at the sounds of Ross and McMachen's voices, fearing for a brief moment that they had come back for him. Even that wasn't enough to make him get up, though. *What was he going to do, anyway? Stand at the back of his cage? If the humans had returned to hurt him, there wasn't much use in resisting. Humans always got their way in the end.*

"Twenty-four hundred parts per million," said Ross. *Skip.*

"The board will be happy to hear it!" *Skip.*

"Turn it up, then."

"...we're actually done for today, sir. We should maintain—"

"We're on a schedule here, Dr. Ross. The board wants the product out by the end of the year. We're going to need to keep going until we get some results."

One of the humans in the hallway whispered an expletive just before the audio cut off. EK shuddered, and heard HK do the same in her cage.

Ghost spoke up, her voice suddenly just outside the door. "Sentinel. The phone worked. We'll need to add this footage to the rest."

"Yeah, I heard." Sentinel sounded grim. "Back it up when you get home and send me a copy."

Ghost sighed. "The dogs are supposed to be in here. I'm going to go inside and check on them. You're welcome to come if you want."

"Okay," said the human with her. "Do you think they're still...you know, alive?"

"I hope so," said Ghost. "I shouldn't have left them here."

"You had to. We needed that footage—"

"Is it worth it, though? Risking their safety for the sake of the investigation?"

"We don't have homes for all of them yet either, Ghost. You know we have to have those first. Come on, *you* always tell *me* I can't blame myself for things out of my control."

"I guess so. But what if that's just an excuse for getting footage? I can't help but wonder if we're doing the right thing when we make these decisions."

"That's why the rest of us trust you. It's why you should trust yourself more, too. You know when to act, but you also never stop weighing the consequences."

The only response was the sound of the door opening.

EK-230 stared at the two figures who slipped into the room. He hoped they could smell the betrayal he felt. *Where were you?* He thought. *I needed you. Why weren't you there?*

Ghost set her light on a counter, casting a dim yellow glow over the room. A strange mixture of concern and relief was written across her face, and she immediately rushed to HK's cage.

"Poor girl. Are you okay?"

Metal scraped against metal as Ghost pulled the pan from under HK's cage. "I'm so sorry you're sick, puppies. I'll clean this up for you, okay?"

She carried the pan to the sink and began rinsing the vomit out. Her companion followed suit with FK's pan, prompting an introduction.

"This is Cobalt," Ghost said as she moved onto EK's cage. "She's here to help."

Despite being at least a few years younger than Caitlyn, Cobalt must have been the biggest human EK had ever seen. She was even taller than Jansson. Thick layers of muscle and fat moved under her biosecurity suit, and EK found himself wondering if she was big enough to carry Ghost. Her skin had an amber tone to it, and the hair on her head was so dark that it absorbed what little light the room had to offer. Some features—like her voice, or the sprinkling of stubble around her chin—might have led EK to mistake her for a boy. Ghost had clearly said *she* though.

Cobalt waved as she turned from the sink.

"Hi puppers." She slid FK's pan back into place. "My name's actually just Sophia."

Ghost gave Cobalt—Sophia—a quizzical look. Sophia simply shrugged and returned to the sink with GK's pan.

"I'm not going to use a fake name anymore," she explained. "It just makes me feel silly. And I kind of associate it with my deadname."

Ghost nodded. "Okay, that's cool."

Ghost slid the clean pan back under EK's cage, and he struggled to his feet. He already felt a little better without the scent of vomit in every breath, and he realized how *thirsty* he was. The burning in his throat had been overshadowed by nausea, but it was certainly still there, and the lukewarm water in his bowl felt as soothing as a gentle rain. Or, at least what he imagined a gentle rain would feel like.

After Sophia replaced GK's pan, the two humans simply stood there, watching for a very long time. EK was starting to wonder if something was wrong when Ghost finally broke the silence.

"You can see how much they've all been throwing up," she said, pointing the camera around the room. "These tests are obviously making them sick, but that doesn't seem to matter to the people doing it."

Ghost lowered the camera and looked at the dogs. "I brought a few treats for you. Have you ever had treats before?"

She reached into her pocket and held a few tiny squares out to EK. He sniffed warily at the squares, and then cocked his head to the side in confusion. They certainly *looked* like any other kind of food, but they smelled different. *Was Ghost trustworthy enough to take food from?*

EK's stomach rumbled, which he took as a sign that he should eat the "treats." He hadn't been hungry since leaving the lab that morning, but he needed food, and Ghost seemed like one of the more trustworthy humans he'd met. He only nibbled at the first treat, but then he hastily gobbled down the rest. *They were delicious! Crunchy and salty, and so much more flavorful than normal food!* He sniffed at Ghost's hand for more, but she just laughed and scratched his head.

"We have to leave some for your friends, buddy!"

She continued scratching his head while she handed a few treats to HK, and EK found himself wishing Ghost would stay forever. Things were always better when Ghost visited, and so much worse when she was gone. *She must have had a good reason for being gone when they needed her,* EK decided. *Maybe it was time to forgive her.*

Ghost smirked at Sophia before crossing behind EK's cage to feed FK and GK. "These are actually cat treats, but Ollie seems to like them way more than the dog treats I get for him."

"Looks like they're universally likeable," Sophia mused. "That's gonna put the dog treat companies out of business."

Ghost started to say something, but a sudden heaving in EK's stomach drowned out whatever it was. A slurry of treats and water came rushing up his throat, forcing its way out of his mouth and falling straight into the pan beneath his cage. He stared at the mess miserably. *Those treats had been good. Why did they have to go away?*

Only a moment later, HK began throwing up *her* treats. The humans exchanged a glance, then rushed to comfort the dogs. Ghost pulled out EK's tray to wash it again.

"I'm so sorry, babies," she said. "I wasn't thinking. I didn't mean to make you sick again! I guess I was hoping treats would cheer you up, not make your tummies hurt!"

"Sorry," Sophia echoed as she pulled out HK's tray.

"We're going to get you out of here soon," said Ghost. "I promise. We just have to find two more homes and the last bit of money we need to take you to the vet. Then you can stop feeling so sick, I promise. Just hang in there, puppies."

Chapter 6

EK-230 breathed a sigh of relief when the sad-eyed man appeared in the doorway. His arrival always meant the end of the day, which meant the risk of going back to the lab was gone for a while.

Three surprisingly uneventful days had passed since the incident with Mr. McMachen. The daily walks were the only exciting thing that happened, but EK had been thrilled to find that they were a little longer than usual. Caitlyn had even lingered to pet him after the walk that morning. She'd seemed almost ready to cry for a moment, but then she smiled, told him she loved him, and moved on to HK's cage.

EK felt a pang in his heart as he remembered the look on Caitlyn's face. *What was wrong with her?* Caitlyn had been one of the better humans, and he hated the idea of something making her sad. He hoped she'd be happy again when he saw her next.

Jansson had stopped by that afternoon, which sent EK into a near panic for several agonizing moments. All she did was hang a small tag on each cage though. Then she left without the slightest hint that anyone was going to the lab.

Maybe she wasn't really that bad after all, EK thought. *Maybe he had misjudged her.*

It was these tags that caught the sad-eyed man's sad eyes when he came in for cleaning. He paused in front of HK's cage, then set his supplies on the ground before grabbing the tag and squinting at it. He did the same with EK's tag, and then GK's, the furrow in his brow deepening each time.

The man abruptly went to the door and looked up and down the hallway. Then he shut the door tight, pulled a phone from his pocket, and dialed. He returned to HK's cage while it rang, holding the tag between his thumb and forefinger.

"Hello?" It took a moment for EK to recognize Ghost's voice over the phone.

"It is Emilio," said the sad-eyed man. "When will you come for the dogs?"

"We're planning to get them out sometime next week. That's when the monthly donations come in, so we'll have enough money to get them to the vet. I have a feeling at least a few will need treatment, and I want us to be able to give it to them."

Emilio shook his head, suddenly agitated. "No. No. It is too long. Come *now.*"

"I…" said Ghost. "Is something wrong?"

Emilio pinched the tag on HK's cage, shaking it as if to emphasize his words.

"Next week is too long. The tags say they are killed Friday. *Tomorrow!*"

There was a long silence on the other end of the line, broken only by Ghost whispering something under her breath.

"Okay," she finally said. "I'll figure something out. Thank you, Emilio. Leave the doors unlocked for us tonight."

Emilio nodded and hung up the phone. Then he turned to the dogs and sighed.

"We will fix this. You will be okay."

EK nuzzled Emilio's hand through the bars of the cage. He was glad that a sense of relief seemed to have come over the man. He didn't like it when his favorite humans were upset, and his spirits were lifted significantly by the idea that Ghost had fixed whatever was bothering Emilio.

***

It was much later than usual when Ghost—it had to have been Ghost—came through the door of Flatiron Life Labs. EK had memorized the slight limping pattern of her footsteps, and it didn't take long for him to recognize Sophia's heavy footfalls as well. The two extra pairs of feet accompanying them were a mystery, but EK suspected he'd find out who they belonged to soon enough.

He wasn't wrong. After a quick trip upstairs, the footsteps returned. Ghost had apparently decided she was done with all the secrecy, and EK found himself blinking in blinding overhead lights as she stepped into the room. *That was different. She hadn't ever turned the lights on before.*

The second major difference was that Ghost was accompanied by three humans. Sophia was one of them, but EK didn't recognize the others. One stood just behind Sophia, and was only slightly older than she was. He wore thick black-

rimmed glasses, and his hair was short and neat. The boy—
man? He was something between the two—held himself in a
clean and professional way, but something about the look in
his eyes told EK he hadn't always been so polished.

Behind him, another...EK struggled for a moment to
identify whether the last member of the group was male or
female. Then he decided it didn't really matter, and settled on
"human." The human had olive skin and dark eyes that drank
in the room with such detail, EK wondered if they could see
things his eyes couldn't. A thick, shaggy swirl of dark hair
covered the top of the human's head, cut so it only barely
missed covering those deep, dark eyes.

The man with glasses spoke first. "Okay, so how does
this work?"

EK instantly recognized the voice. *Sentinel.*

Ghost shrugged. "Pretty straightforward. We take
them out, take them to the vet in case they need treatment—
they probably will—and document the whole thing. And again,
this rescue is *open.* We show our faces to the camera openly to
demonstrate that we know we're in the right, even if the laws
don't reflect that yet. Harley will take the front. Follow them
on the way out. I'll bring up the rear so I can film."

"Hey Mattie?" said the human with dark eyes. *Harley,*
EK thought. It was the only name he hadn't connected to a
person yet.

"Yeah?"

"Before we turn the cameras on, I want to make sure
you're okay with this. The rest of us have been through it
before, but I wanted to check with you one last time. You've
already saved all four of these dogs by tracking down donors

on such short notice, and it's totally understandable if you don't want to be publicly involved. You don't want to risk getting kicked out of school."

Sentinel—*Mattie*—shrugged. "I mean, they probably won't bring charges, right?"

"Probably not," said Ghost. "The Biomedical Sciences Department decided to press charges when we got Vera out of UBW, but that backfired by giving the story lots of extra media attention. The student body got pretty upset once they started hearing about it. Lots of petitions and sit-ins and stuff. Anyway, I went to jail for three weeks, but a postdoc left the university and the head researcher ended up in an early retirement. I almost feel bad—"

"Except they were screwing rods into cats' skulls," Harley interrupted.

Ghost gave a wan smile. "Yeah. Not that bad. That's the only time I've been charged. We've never done a rescue in this county though, so I don't know how predictable we can count on the DA being. It's a possibility."

Mattie thought for a moment, then said, "I'll risk it. I want to be here. Besides, I told myself I wouldn't *completely* sell out in college. If I'd known about this place a few years ago, I probably would have burned it to the ground."

"Right," Ghost nodded. "But that's not what we do. Let's get on with the plan."

Ghost crossed to EK's cage and reached inside. EK happily licked at her fingers, which were still sticky with traces of some kind of sauce. *Ghost was here, so everything would be good for a while.* The longer EK thought about it, the more excited he got. *Maybe she had more treats!*

Ghost was clearly preoccupied though, and she had other matters to attend to. After a few quick scratches behind EK's ears, she stepped away from the cage.

"Sophia?" she asked. "You're good with this too? There's public video of you doing the last one with me, so if there are charges, they could be harsher this time."

Sophia simply nodded and gave Ghost a quiet, "Yeah. Let's go."

"Okay."

Ghost sighed and turned on each of her cameras—one on her forehead, another strapped to her chest. Harley followed suit with a handheld camera, and Sophia began filming with her phone. Little red lights on each camera winked at EK, briefly hypnotizing him. Then the whole room slid into the quietest kind of chaos imaginable.

Ghost started fiddling with the latch on EK's cage, and Sophia did the same for HK's. It was only then that EK became aware of his sister's nervous panting. That gave him pause. *Was HK right to be worried?* He'd been so focused on the humans, he hadn't thought about what they might be up to. *They seemed kind, but did he really know them? What if it was all just for another trip to the lab?*

A harsh *click* sounded from the back of the room, followed by Mattie whispering, "There are handles on the top and the bottom. You have to get both at the same time."

Three more clicks sounded in quick succession. Still more excited than nervous, EK wagged his tail as the door to his cage swung open. *Ghost was taking him somewhere! For a walk? To a secret stash of treats?* EK nearly leapt into her arms, and a silent grin spread across her face. She cradled him and opened her mouth to speak, but a frustrated series of whispers from Sophia cut her off.

"No, no, come here. It's okay sweetie, I promise. Come on. Please?"

EK glanced toward Sophia and saw HK cowering in the corner of her cage. She allowed Sophia to scratch her head, but every time the human tried to pick her up, she flipped and flopped until she slipped back into the safety of her cage. That was how HK had always been. A known situation—even a bad one—was better than the unknown.

It wasn't until after Harley and Mattie returned with GK and FK in their arms that Sophia managed to coax HK out. None of the humans seemed to know where the dogs' leashes were, so they never let them down to the floor. Instead, they hugged EK and his siblings close, whispering reassurances like "it's okay, we're not here to hurt you" and "everything's going to be okay, buddy."

Ghost gave EK-230 a few more scratches before sweeping her gaze—and her camera—over her teammates' faces.

"Okay," she said. "Everyone good to go?"

The humans nodded, and Harley headed for the door with Mattie and Sophia close behind. Ghost panned the room one last time, pausing for a moment to make sure her camera caught the tag on EK's cage. Then she followed her friends into the hall, flicking off the light and tugging the door shut with her elbow.

EK did his best not to squirm as he and Ghost bobbed up and down behind the rest of the humans. The journey wasn't long, but he certainly would have preferred to walk instead of being carried. Being carried around by humans hadn't exactly ended well in the past, and it made him nervous. For once, he found himself glad that the hallway was so short.

The front doors squealed as Harley pushed them open, and the cool wave of air that washed over EK smelled better than anything he could have imagined. He couldn't *wait* to be out there. To follow his siblings through those doors and finally, *finally* be outside. *This was his dream!* He was going *outside,* and if that meant he had to be carried, he didn't mind.

To EK's annoyance, Ghost paused less than a single step away from the world outside. He squirmed anxiously as she shifted him to one arm, but her grip was far too strong to escape. EK finally had to resign himself to waiting while Ghost pulled the camera off her head and turned it toward herself. A shaft of light from an outside streetlamp illuminated her face, and EK briefly wondered if he could *smell* the glee shining in her eyes.

"Flatiron Life Labs: my name is Annie Collins, and you're done hurting these dogs. We're taking them somewhere safe."

Chapter 7

EK got exactly one breath of crisp night air before everything went wrong.

"Hide!" someone hissed. *Harley.*

Before EK knew it, they were huddled under a nearby bush. Ghost covered his entire body with hers, draping her arms around him and pressing him close to the ground. It was too dark for sight to be any use, so EK had to make sense of the situation with his ears. He could hear all three of his siblings breathing, along with the more anxious breath of the four humans. There was the rustle of leaves in the bushes and the beating of Ghost's heart, but the rest of the world was silent. It was several moments before Harley spoke again.

"Headlights. We only made it a few steps before someone pulled into the parking lot. I don't know if they saw us."

Ghost—*no, Annie. Her name was Annie now*—tensed. Her heart beat so hard against EK's back, he wondered if it might come right out of her chest. "Security? There's never been anyone here before!"

No one replied. They simply waited in the bushes, breathing and listening. And then EK heard the footsteps. One human, heavy and tall. *But not in a hurry...the human hadn't seen them!*

That could change at any moment, though. Slow as they were, the footsteps were getting closer. They stepped onto the sidewalk, and then passed by the bushes so close EK was certain they'd be caught. But the human only ever broke rhythm to pause at the door and then turn back the way he'd come.

Annie let out a quiet exhale as the footsteps retreated, and EK realized he'd been holding his own breath. Everything was calm for a while, and the footsteps had nearly returned to the car when Mattie let out a flurry of panicked whispers.

"No, hey, no! Shit, *shit.*"

EK poked his face out from under Annie's arms just in time to see FK, always the adventurous one, worm her way out of the bush. She trotted down the sidewalk, stopping occasionally to sniff at the pavement. Mattie moved to sneak out and grab her, but the security guard spotted her first, and Mattie sunk back down to the safety of the bushes.

EK's heart pounded as the uniformed man marched toward FK. *This was bad. Didn't she understand? Run! Get away from there!*

"Where did you come from?" the security guard asked.

EK watched in horror as the uniformed man picked up his sister and began searching for identifying marks. He shot Annie a nervous glance, hoping she'd have a plan. Annie was frozen though, eyes wide and mouth open.

"Did you get out of the facility?" asked the guard. "How did that happen?"

He turned back to his car, FK still securely trapped in his grip.

"Come on, we're going to go call the building manager."

EK squirmed in Annie's arms, but she held him down. He would have screamed if he had a voice. *Don't let him take you back, FK! You can't go back!*

Mattie apparently came to a decision, and after whispering "shit" three more times, he tore his biosecurity suit off and ran from the bush. He slowed to a jog once he made it halfway to the security guard, raising his hands in relief.

"Oh good, I'm so glad you found her! She got out through the front door, and she's so quick, I didn't know if I'd ever see her again!"

The guard eyed Mattie suspiciously. "This is your dog?"

"Yes," Mattie replied.

"Well, this is private property. You shouldn't be here."

"Yes sir, sorry. I was just trying to follow her so I didn't lose her. We'll be going home right away."

For a moment, the guard appeared ready to hand FK over. Then his voice took on a hard, suspicious edge.

"What's her name?"

The question caught Mattie off guard. "Uh…what?"

"What is your dog's name?"

Harley let out the tiniest of sighs. It was beyond quiet, but enough to warrant a glance from EK. Those deep, dark eyes were fixed on the unfolding scene, taking it all in. Analyzing. Thinking. Harley didn't even blink as they pushed GK toward Annie.

"Oh, yeah. Her name…"

Harley's eyes flashed. Within a heartbeat, GK had joined EK under Annie's protective arms. A quick "hang onto him" was all that could be heard before Harley ran out of the bush, whipping off a canvas belt and looping it through itself three times. It all happened so fast that EK realized he hadn't even seen Harley take off their biosecurity suit.

Harley started calling out after only a few steps. "Flo! Flo-ooh! Here girl! Flo-oooh!"

Harley paused, pretending to spot the security guard for the first time. "Oh, you found her!"

Mattie recovered himself and turned to the guard. "Her name is Flo."

Harley moved so fast, the guard didn't even have time to react. They ran straight up to him, slipping the belt over FK's neck and cinching it down tight. In the same motion, they pulled her from his arms and cradled her in their own.

"There you go, girl. That's the last time we let you go to bed without your collar on."

"Come on," Harley said to Mattie. "Let's get home. We've lost enough sleep already."

Harley turned without another word and marched back the way they had come. Mattie offered the security guard one last glance and nodded nervously.

"Thanks again for finding her, sir," he said. Then he ran after Harley.

FK, Harley, and Mattie disappeared behind Flatiron Life Labs. EK tried to follow them, but Annie and Sophia made him wait while the security guard swept the property again. It took so long, EK was certain the sun would come up before the guard left. He took a slow lap around the entire building, then aimlessly wandered the parking lot, strolling back and forth and back and forth before finally leaning against his car and lighting a cigarette. The blue glow of a phone screen cast an eerie light on his face. He stared intently at the device, only looking up to chuckle to himself or take a drag on the cigarette.

It was ages before the guard finally put his cigarette out and drove away, and ages still before Annie and Sophia allowed anyone to move. EK could barely even hear the sound of the guard's engine fading in the distance when Annie *finally* spoke.

"Let's go."

She gathered Harley and Mattie's biosecurity suits from a tangle of branches and stuffed them deep into her own. Then she scooped EK and his brother into her arms and set off across the parking lot, jogging opposite the direction Harley, Mattie, and FK had gone. EK thought that was strange. He wondered for a moment if Annie was lost, but Sophia followed without questioning the decision. He didn't think they could possibly *both* be lost, so he decided he'd just wait and see what the humans had planned.

They jogged down a series of streets before finally reaching a car parked in a dimly lit residential area. Annie paused by the car, waiting for a panting Sophia to climb in the back seat with HK. Then she passed EK and GK to Sophia and shut the door. It was crowded, so EK supposed it was a good thing that Annie picked a spot in the driver's seat instead of the back. She started the car, then leaned back and took a few deep breaths before pulling away from the curb.

There were so many turns that EK lost track of them after only a short time. He wondered again if Annie had gotten them lost. Each road led to another, but darkness obscured far too much of the world to see many details. *How could Annie possibly navigate this endless maze? How could she even see?* She must have figured it out somehow though, and managed to stop the car in the exact spot Harley, Mattie, and FK were waiting. *Annie was smart!* EK was so excited to see his companions safe and sound, he barely even noticed the extra crowding when Mattie slid into the back seat.

Everything was silent as Harley climbed into the passenger seat. FK settled in on their lap, still wearing the canvas belt with the letters "FLOW" printed over a small wave design on its surface. Annie drove off without a word. EK found the sound of tires on pavement oddly comforting, and the gentle motion of the car combined with Sophia's protective hand against his back lulled him into a daze. He nearly jumped when Annie finally broke the silence.

"I'm sorry. I should have handled that. Talking if we got caught was always supposed to be my responsibility, and I froze up."

She took her eyes off the road for a quick glance at her knee, then continued.

"And I'm sorry for putting all of you in that situation. I should have discovered security a long time ago, and I want to own that mistake. I—"

"It's okay," Mattie interrupted. "I let her get away in the first place."

"We're all here," said Harley. "Let's skip the blame game and just focus on getting to the vet. We said we'd meet her there at four, and we're running late."

Everyone was quiet again after that, and the only sounds were the whine of the engine and the hum of tires on the road.

Chapter 8

The sunrise was so...*incredible*. He hadn't ever seen one before. There hadn't been any windows to look through in the room at Flatiron Life Labs, and the daily walks only happened long after the sun was up. Everything had changed, though. The dogs were free to look through any window they liked on the ride home from the vet, and everything already looked better than before. He even had a brand new name: Echo. *Much better than EK-230.*

The night had been anything but short. Mattie left for home after they arrived at the vet, but Harley and Sophia had been there the whole time, keeping the dogs calm while Annie sorted out the logistics. Echo hadn't exactly liked the vet—it reminded him too much of the lab—so he stayed on Harley's lap for almost the entire visit. And Harley had comforted him, patting his back or holding him close, even covering him with a jacket when he got cold.

Harley was different from the other humans Echo had met. Most humans seemed to style themselves in ways that painted them as either male or female, but Harley blurred the two together. Traits pointing toward one side were often countered by something pointing to another. Many traits didn't seem to point toward male *or* female, but something different entirely. And Harley was always called "they" rather than "he" or "she" like the other humans. Echo had pondered this matter briefly before deciding Harley must simply be a type of human he hadn't met before. It seemed likely that there were more than two kinds. After all, it would be foolish to think he could know every possible category of human without meeting them all first.

Harley patted Echo's back, and he shot them an excited glance before returning his gaze to the window. Annie was busy driving, and Sophia was asleep in the back seat with the rest of Echo's siblings. He didn't mind that. It meant he got Harley all to himself, and Harley was a good human.

Harley's voice wasn't as soft as Annie's, and their personality was much more reserved. Echo knew they both cared, though. When the vet had given him a shot, his sides shook so hard that he could barely stand. Needles had become more and more terrifying since the incident with the mice. Harley seemed to understand this, though. They held his trembling sides the whole time, promised him over and over that he was safe. And they were right. They *kept* him safe.

Harley had also been the one to find Echo's new name. Flo had gotten her name outside the lab of course, and Sophia had named GK "Jakey" on the way to the vet. The humans didn't seem to know whether or not the dogs had ever been addressed by their numbers, but Sophia seemed to think a hint of familiarity might help them adjust to their new names. She named HK "Hollie" and suggested "Eekay" for Echo, but Annie thought that name was a little *too* close. She said she didn't want to make him carry his number everywhere he went, and suggested Emmet instead. It only took Sophia a moment's glance at Echo to proclaim that he was definitely *not* an Emmet.

Echo had listened to all this from Harley's lap, a little less than half-asleep. He'd actually been startled when Harley spoke up, because their voice seemed to come from every direction at once. It wasn't until he looked up that he realized Harley's head was resting on his.

"EK-two-three-oh," Harley mused. "What about Echo? That carries a few of the same phonetic sounds."

"Echo?" Sophia asked.

"Echo."

The new name would certainly be an adjustment from EK, and it felt foreign and strange in his ears. But it also felt *good.* It was a name that was *meant* to be a name, not just an identifier for Jansson's tablet.

Annie nodded slowly and asked, "Do you like Echo, buddy?"

She had reached down to pet him then, but he ducked away before she could. He didn't want *any* human touching his face. Not even Annie. It was just too risky. He didn't want her to think he was unhappy though, so he gave her fingers a few quick licks. *Echo was nice. Echo would do just fine.*

Annie parked the car and set to work on waking the back seat's occupants. Flo and Hollie woke up fairly quickly, but Jakey and Sophia were an entirely different story. Echo, Flo, and Hollie had already followed Harley all the way to the living room by the time the others stumbled inside. Sophia yawned and plopped down on the couch, absently scratching at the now-prominent stubble under her chin while Jakey settled onto her lap.

Annie smiled. "Do you want a ride home? I can take you and Jakey before everyone else gets here."

"That's okay," Sophia yawned again. She glanced down at Jakey, who was already well on his way back to sleep. "I want to watch them go out on the grass. And besides, Jakey probably wants a little more time with his friends before he comes home with me."

Jakey snorted and relieved himself on Sophia's lap. She jumped up immediately, startling Jakey so much that he leapt away with pee still trailing behind him. Echo expected Sophia to be angry, but she seemed more embarrassed than anything else. She glanced from her soaked pants to Annie and Harley, and then to the couch. A horrified expression crept across her face.

"I am so, so sorry."

"It's—" Annie put a hand to her mouth to stifle a laugh.

"It's okay," said Harley. They shot Annie a look, which only made her laugh harder. "No one is ever potty-trained when we first rescue them. That's why we have a steam cleaner."

Annie finally pulled herself together enough to speak. "Sorry…guess I'm just slaphappy from being up all night! Come on, let's throw those in the wash. I'll get you something clean to wear."

Echo tried to get a sense of his new surroundings while Annie and Sophia were gone, but the house was far too chaotic for exploring. The doorbell rang three times in just a few short moments, and each new human Harley let inside insisted on meeting the dogs. Echo had already forgotten all of their names by the time Annie and Sophia returned and suggested going to the backyard.

All of the humans except for Annie and Harley shuffled outside, which helped things quiet down. It should have also lessened the confusion, but the humans immediately turned to assembling the dogs near the back door and debating letting them out before the newspaper's photographer arrived. Echo gathered from the debate that "newspapers" were useful for getting other humans to hear stories, and that other newspapers tended to pay more attention to stories when one newspaper had already published something. Pictures were very important for all of this, though Echo couldn't figure out exactly how they fit in.

Echo shook himself. *So many words.* It was difficult to piece meanings together when he only understood a fraction of what the humans said. All the talk was making his head hurt. Fortunately, the newspaper photographer arrived a few moments later, settling the debate. Echo watched him exit through the back door with Harley. Then Annie knelt down and looked at each of the dogs in turn.

"Okay puppies," she said. "Are you ready to go exploring?"

Echo was still trying to figure out what she meant when she pulled the door open and urged them into the yard.

Outside! Echo could hardly contain himself. His tail wagged so hard it shook his whole body, which made it surprisingly difficult to navigate the short drop from the doorway to the patio. He stumbled briefly on the way down, but he was too excited to care much about that. There were smells and sounds everywhere. *Fresh plants. A breeze. Bugs. Birds. Human voices. The click-click-click of a camera.* Echo had been outside exactly four times since the previous night's rescue, but those trips had always been brief, and he'd always been carried by a human. *Not anymore.* He could finally walk around all by himself, free to go wherever he wanted.

Annie jogged out into the grass and knelt just in front of the other humans. "Come here, puppies!"

Jakey went first, bounding off the patio and into Annie's waiting arms. He kicked his feet up every step of the way, seemingly delighted with the feel of the ground. Hollie followed more carefully, padding gently across the yard and stopping for a sniff every few steps. Echo followed her all the way to the edge of the patio, but froze just before touching the grass. An image of dead mice stuck full of pins flashed across his mind, followed by one of Dr. Ross with those awful needles.

Echo eyed the grass suspiciously. The longer he looked, the more the short, sharp blades looked like pins and needles. And there were more than he could count. *This wasn't safe.*

He took a step back, putting some distance between himself and the lawn of needles. Flo raced past him only a moment later, nearly plowing into Jakey before slowing to a more conservative romp. Despite the near collision, she seemed unharmed. In fact, grass didn't seem to cause harm to any of Echo's siblings. Or the humans. Still, he didn't trust it. It *seemed* soft, but he'd seen those mice. Things weren't always what they seemed, and Echo wasn't about to risk jumping into a whole field of potentially sharp objects.

"What's wrong, bud?"

The voice startled Echo until he realized it belonged to Harley. They reached down to pet him, and he whined before backing farther away from the grass. He did *not* want to get poked.

Harley sat down next to him, and together they watched Echo's siblings play. It didn't take long for them to tire out, since the only exercise they'd ever had were Caitlyn's pitifully short walks. Still, Echo found himself glad when the humans carried his siblings back inside. It was embarrassing to be so afraid in front of everyone, even for a short time.

After the door had safely closed behind everyone else, Harley motioned Annie over.

"What's wrong?" Annie asked. "Are you scared, buddy?"

"I think he might be a little overwhelmed," Harley said. "I figured trying to coax him out into the yard can wait for later."

"Later…" Annie nodded. "So you're going to be staying with us, Echo?"

"I think that would be best," said Harley. "Sophia's taking Jakey, and we only found two other homes since it was such short notice. I know we were planning to just foster one of them, but…could he just live with us permanently? He's really scared, and we've already connected, and I think he trusts me. We have enough room for him, right?"

Annie thought for a moment, then smiled. "Yeah, we can make room."

She reached toward Echo's head, then seemed to remember he didn't like head scratches and switched to his back. "We'll give you all the time you need to adjust, bud. And we'll keep you safe. No more labs, no more experiments. I promise."

She smiled at Harley. "You know, usually it's *me* begging *you* to take in another animal. You're right though, he does seem attached to you."

"Yeah." Harley patted Echo's back. "So…do you want to be part of our family, buddy?"

Echo licked Harley's hand and led his new humans back into the safety of the house.

Chapter 9

Echo felt much safer inside. The irony of that wasn't lost on him, since going outside was something he'd always dreamed of. But after finally leaving the lab, Echo just wanted to feel safe and secure. Outside could wait.

The humans began to leave just after Echo got back inside, and his siblings slowly disappeared with them. Jakey, now wide-awake, left with a yawning Sophia. Flo went home with a gray-haired couple, and Hollie was adopted by a mother and her daughter. Hollie had seemed wary of the daughter at first, but she warmed up to the small human after a short time.

Goodbye HK—Hollie, Echo thought. He'd miss his siblings, and he'd miss her most of all. Even if they hadn't had much time together at the lab, Echo felt a special bond with Hollie. They'd lived right next to each other after all, and he'd been falling asleep to the sound of her breathing for as long as he could remember.

Annie claimed there wasn't any need for Echo to be sad to see his siblings go. She promised he'd see them again, and that they could have something called playdates. Still, it hurt to be without them. They were the only friends he ever really had. He decided he would trust the humans, though.

They promised to introduce him to his "new family" after showing him around the house, so he padded along for the tour.

The living room was easy enough to remember—that's where they had all gone when they first went inside. It contained a couch, a desk, a TV, a large window, and the front door. The next room over was the kitchen, which contained a small table and the back door, along with quite a few cupboards and appliances. Echo's favorite part of the kitchen was the way his nails click-clacked against the wood floor. The ever-present bowl of food by the door was a close second, though.

A small hallway at the end of the kitchen split off in three directions. Straight ahead was a closet, which Annie opened to reveal an assortment of coats and cleaning supplies. She closed the closet door again before Echo could get much sniffing in, but he figured he could always return later. To the right of the closet was a large bathroom, which doubled as a laundry room. Echo supposed he'd have to return to that one too, since the stale scents of pee and dryer lint required a much more thorough investigation than he had time for.

The last place the hallway led was up a flight of stairs, which doubled back on itself at a landing halfway up. The second floor of the house was even smaller than the first. There were only three doors at the top of the stairs: a second bathroom, a small office, and Annie and Harley's bedroom. The door to the bedroom was closed, which Harley said was because the rest of the animals were in there. They wanted to have Echo meet them slowly, which he accepted without much complaint.

"Do you want to head down to the living room with him?" Annie asked. "We'll bring everyone else down slowly so they can meet without any freakouts."

Harley started downstairs, then paused. "Let's take a break for breakfast first. Echo might need a little extra time to adjust to the house before meeting anyone new. Plus, I'm sure we're all hungry.

Annie nodded and led the way downstairs. Whatever the humans had for breakfast smelled good, but Echo was more interested in the bowl of food he'd spotted on the tour. *Could that food really be there all the time? No more waiting and going hungry?* He could hardly believe it.

Echo wondered about the differences between the lab and the house all throughout breakfast. Why there were so many windows. Where the walking hallway was. And what the humans meant by "the rest of the family." *More humans, like Harley and Annie? Or more dogs?* Echo couldn't decide which prospect excited him more.

After breakfast, Annie headed back up the stairs while Harley buckled a brand new collar around Echo's neck. Then came a leash and a short walk to the living room, where they waited for what felt like half of the morning.

When Annie finally reappeared, she had a couple of strange creatures in her arms. They were made almost entirely of white fluff, except for their eyes and the pink skin in their ears. The ears themselves were *fascinating*. They were much longer than Echo's, but they pointed up into the air instead of flopping toward the ground. Even more interesting were the creatures' noses. They were constantly moving, twitching up and down and up and down and then suddenly to the side before twitching up and down again. *Like they had minds of their own.*

Harley held Echo back while Annie lowered one of the creatures to the ground.

"Echo, this is Bear." Annie motioned to the creature on the ground, then nodded at the one still in her arms. "And this is Moose. They're *bunnies*, and they're not as big as you, so we have to be very careful with them, okay?"

Bear hesitantly started toward Echo. Instead of walking, he moved in a strange hopping manner, his back legs constantly playing catch-up with the front. *What a fascinating creature.*

Bear stopped just under Echo's nose and stared for a moment before sniffing at him. Echo drew back, but cautiously returned the sniff once he realized the bunny meant no harm. *Bunnies smelled soft. And warm. And more than a little stressed out.*

When Annie set the other bunny—Moose—down, he didn't move. He just sat there, cloudy eyes fixed on the couch. Aside from his breathing and the twitching in his nose, the bunny's ears seemed to be the only thing capable of moving. But they were *moving.* Swiveling. Listening. Watching, almost like they could see. As Echo approached, the ears swiveled to look directly at him. Then Moose turned and sniffed at his entire face, smelling almost every inch of it. It seemed excessive, but Echo didn't mind too much. He liked the bunnies. They were small and soft, and didn't seem to want to hurt him. *Those were all very good qualities.*

"Well," Annie said wryly. "It's going much better than when we introduced them to Vera."

Annie knelt by Echo's side, but Harley remained standing, leash held tightly in a protective manner. Echo stared at them for several moments, wondering if they were protecting the bunnies from *him*. He found that more than a little upsetting. *They were small, yes, but didn't Harley trust him?*

Annie placed a hand on Echo's back, distracting him from his thoughts. "Good boy. We always have to be very gentle with the bunnies."

"Moose here is blind," Annie said. "His hearing is pretty good, but sometimes he runs into things he can't hear, like walls.

"Bear can see well enough to get around, but he has a hard time recognizing anything more than a few inches from his face, so he might get in your personal bubble sometimes. Actually, they both might. They're not trying to bother you though, okay?"

Echo liked how thoroughly Annie and Harley explained everything. Even though he only understood fragments of what they said, he liked being treated like an independent person instead of some kind of lesser being.

"They came from a lab too," said Annie. "They had to deal with different stuff than you did—that's why they're blind—but they get what you've been through. They were actually the first ones I helped save from a lab, way back before Harley and I were even married."

Annie smiled up at Harley, who allowed an amused expression to creep across their face. For the first time, Echo noticed how tall they were. They hadn't seemed very tall next to Sophia, but trying to look all the way up at Harley's face made Echo feel like he was going to fall over.

Annie's expression darkened as she turned back to Moose. "We found all the notes that lab took. It was for some hair and body care company. The stuff they were testing has been known to cause eye damage since the nineties, but I guess it makes hair extra shiny or something. They wanted to use it in their shampoo *so* bad that they had a whole project devoted to finding compounds that could neutralize the damaging effects. By the time we got there, they were almost done with the compound they'd picked for Bear and Moose' group. Obviously, it didn't work. Some degree of partial blindness in five of the rabbits, and total blindness in three more. I can only imagine how many others they blinded and then threw in the garbage during their other tests.

"Only one bunny got out without eye damage, so we assume he was the experimental control. I adopted Bear and Moose, and the rest of their siblings went to other homes."

Annie fell silent and started rubbing Moose's back. Echo sat down, unsure of what to do besides stare at the bunnies and humans. It was several moments before Harley finally broke the silence.

"Let's take a little break so Echo can get used to the idea of the bunnies. Then I'll go get Ollie so Echo can meet him."

Annie nodded and kissed Moose's head. "Okay, good idea. He's probably dying to come downstairs anyway."

Everyone sat quietly for several moments before Harley got up, disappeared around the corner, and climbed the stairs. Echo expected them to return a while later with another bunny, but only a few heartbeats passed before he heard shouting.

"Ollie, slow down. Ollie, sit! HEY!"

Four clumsy paws clambered down the stairs, followed immediately by the much quieter sound of Harley's feet. Echo tensed and looked to Annie for some cue to flee, but she just grinned and scooped him up in her arms.

A dog at least three times Echo's size came skidding around the corner then, claws clattering against the wood floor. Harley rounded the corner only a heartbeat later, still shouting at the dog to stop. He didn't seem to hear though, and Bear and Moose fled under the desk as he came crashing into the room. He only stopped when his nose bumped up against Annie's leg, and then he stood in front of her, whining and wagging his tail until Harley finally caught up.

Harley grabbed the dog's collar and pulled him back, scolding him for not listening. After making the big dog sit and telling him to calm down several times, they finally glanced up at Annie.

"Okay, you can put him down now."

Annie gently lowered Echo back to the ground, and Harley allowed the big dog to inch forward. He was already sniffing at Echo at least a tail-length away, and he kept going from there. Echo tried to greet the dog several times, but that was difficult to do when he was being sniffed everywhere. It was all a little invasive. His face, his neck, his face again, his paws, his tail, his face…Echo felt dizzy by the time the big dog actually slowed down enough for a proper greeting.

"Echo, this is Ollie," said Annie. "Ollie, this is Echo. He's going to be your little brother."

Even with his massive size, Ollie wasn't nearly as tall as the humans. His coat was shaggy and brown, except for a few white patches on his face and a hint of gray around his muzzle. He licked Echo several times, and Echo hesitantly licked back. *He seemed friendly enough. Like a clumsy but gentle giant.* Still, Echo decided he'd have to be careful around this one. He'd hate to be in the way when the big dog went charging down the stairs.

Annie turned to Echo. "Sorry. Ollie's been around the longest, but he still gets overexcited every time he meets someone new. He'll calm down soon, right Ollie?"

When Ollie did eventually calm down, he wandered over to the couch and splayed his legs across the cushions. He rested his head against the armrest, but kept his eyes open instead of going to sleep. *Just watching,* Echo realized. *Just like any other dog might.*

Echo had relaxed again by the time Harley went upstairs to get Aspen, who was quite unlike any other creature he had met. She walked on only two legs, and had feathers instead of fur. What's more, what should have been her mouth ended in a hard, curved structure that frightened Echo. Just above the almost-mouth, a dark pair of eyes peered up at him.

He sniffed at the creature—a "chicken," she was called—after Harley set her down. She cocked her head to the side and eyed Echo, then suddenly lurched forward with an open mouth.

Echo yelped and leaped away. *She bit him! He hadn't even done anything, and she bit him!*

He nearly yelped again when he felt a hand on his back, but relaxed when he realized it was just Annie. The bite hadn't been hard. It had actually been quite soft and curious, almost like a greeting. *But what kind of greeting was a bite?*

"It's okay, buddy," Annie said. "She isn't trying to hurt you. She just uses her beak to learn about anyone she meets."

He wouldn't ever admit it after the way he had reacted, but Echo realized Annie was probably right. The bite hadn't really hurt. Emboldened by Annie's protective hand, he leaned forward to sniff at Aspen's face again. He flinched when she cocked her head to the side, but she didn't peck him that time. Instead, she simply wandered off to inspect the baseboard on a nearby wall.

Echo watched the bird cautiously while Annie explained that he had to be gentle around her, too. *She didn't seem all that threatening, but...*Echo still wasn't sure. This would be another one to keep a close eye on.

"Aspen was going to be killed for meat at a public demonstration on some little farm," said Annie. "Harley heard about it, so they stopped by on their way home from work. A bunch of chickens had already been killed and Aspen was next, but Harley grabbed her while no one was looking."

Aspen was a little scary, but that wasn't any reason to kill her, Echo thought. *What kind of human would do that? Was it Dr. Ross? Dr. Ross might have wanted to put needles in her.* He actually felt sorry for the bird, although he still planned to keep his distance.

The humans decided Echo needed another break, so it was a while before he got to meet Vera. He spent most of his break wandering around the living room, sniffing in corners and testing what he could chew on. Couches, it turned out, were not for chewing. Neither were desks. Tennis balls were, but tennis balls were very big, and his jaws grew tired long before it was time to meet Vera. He spent the rest of the time warily watching the bunnies, who Annie had penned into a corner with a stack of pillows. He wondered if Vera would be as soft and strange as the bunnies.

Vera turned out to be a cat, which meant she was a graceful, grumpy kind of bunny who had short ears and a long tail instead of the other way around. Her eyes were yellow, and she was covered in black fur except for a large, messy patch of white scar tissue on her forehead. She was smaller than Echo, but she was almost able to reach his face when she gave him a wary sniff. *So thin, but tall too.* Echo wondered how she managed to walk around without losing her balance.

After a second look at the cat, Echo noticed something peculiar. Vera had a tattoo inside her ear too—some mix of human symbols partially obscured by fur. It started with a 5, or maybe an S, and then disappeared behind a tuft of fur before ending in a 6. Curious, Echo inched forward to inspect the symbols.

"That's right," Annie said. "Vera has a tattoo, just like you.

"She didn't come from the same lab as you—she was at a university up north a ways—but there was some really nasty stuff going on there. They screwed a big rod into her skull to make it easier to keep her head still during the experiments, but then it got all infected. That's why she has such a big scar on her face.

"The team I was with got six cats out. We knew we had to move fast, but they were already so sick. The vet had to euthanize all of them except Vera and one of her sisters. She said the infections were in their brains, and they would have died within a few days. She said it was the most peaceful way to go, but it was still so hard...I held every one of them while they got the injection. I wanted them to know what it was like to have someone care for them at least once in their lives."

Vera meowed and rubbed against Annie's leg, which brought a weak smile to her face.

"I know, sweetie. I'm glad you're okay, too."

Harley knelt next to Vera and scratched her chin. "We have to be careful with Vera, just like the other small animals. Okay Echo? She gets seizures sometimes—brain damage from her time in the lab. We give her meds for it every night, but she still has fits from time to time, especially when she gets too worked up.

"Researchers can get away with almost anything." They spat out the words with a sudden anger that startled Echo. "No one will regulate them as long as they can find someone else doing something similar. It's a loophole in the laws that govern them."

Echo thought about the experiments Vera had been through, and thought he understood why Harley was angry. *Could it be possible that there were humans even worse than Dr. Ross out there?* The idea made him shudder.

Annie wrapped her arms around Harley for a moment before reaching down to pet Echo. "That's everyone, buddy. Make yourself at home. I know it's a little tight, but it has to be better than that cage. And I promise you're safe here."

Echo trusted her. *He was safe.* He just had to keep reminding himself of that. No more Dr. Ross, or Jansson, or Mr. McMachen. *They were gone. He was safe.*

Chapter 10

Echo was exhausted by the end of his first day at home. He had peed on the floor twice, which for some reason always made the humans rush him outside. The second time it happened, Annie had actually snatched him up before he was even finished. It was a little shocking, to say the least. He understood that they wanted him to go outside to pee, but how they expected him to get there remained a mystery. The back door was about as useful as a wall unless a human opened it, and Annie and Harley were smart enough to know that. At the same time, Ollie seemed to make it work. *How did he do that?*

That particular mystery had occupied Echo off and on for most of the afternoon, but it was far from the only thing that happened. The humans had tried to get him onto the grass again, but he was *not* about to do that. He eventually convinced them to give up. Once back inside, he'd learned that Aspen wasn't "potty trained" either, so she sometimes wore a little cloth diaper around the house. He also learned in a somewhat noisy incident that neither the chicken nor the humans appreciated him trying to take the diaper off.

He'd done a little more searching around the house after that, and found that the laundry room was actually a very pleasant place when the dryer was on. It was a little noisy, sure, but it was warm. He had tried using the little plastic box next to the dryer as a bed, but had been rather rudely awakened when Vera kicked him out so she could poop in it. He didn't use it as a bed again after that.

The closet next to the laundry room smelled like some sort of bottled cleaning solution, so Echo didn't waste much time there. He *hated* cleaning solutions. They smelled like the lab no matter how much citrus the humans added.

He had wandered to the kitchen from there, where Annie and Harley were making dinner. Annie had asked if he wanted some food, and then knelt down with a little white cube.

"He's not gonna want tofu, babe," said Harley.

Echo sniffed at the cube. It smelled of oil and garlic, but only on the side that had browned on the stove. The rest didn't have much of a smell at all. Echo decided to give it a try anyway. *Annie had been right about treats tasting good, after all. She was probably right about tofu too.*

Tofu tasted like it smelled, but it was *squishy!* Echo squeezed it between his gums, testing the way it gave and bounced back. It almost fell out of his mouth when it finally broke, but he managed to keep it in by tossing his head back and swallowing before it could escape. *That was fun!* He panted up at Annie, eagerly awaiting another piece.

Annie gave Harley a smirk. She dropped another piece of tofu for Echo, and then popped one into her own mouth. "Looks like he wants tofu to me!"

"*Okay*," Harley said in feigned annoyance. "Ollie hates it, so you can't blame me for looking at it empirically."

"And *you* can't blame me for being right!"

Annie twirled over to the spice cupboard, spatula still in hand. Harley rolled their eyes, but Echo couldn't smell any real annoyance. He actually thought he detected a hint of amusement on their face. *Humans played in such strange ways.*

At the end of the day, Echo found himself splayed out next to Ollie on the living room floor. Annie and Harley were cuddling on the couch, half watching TV, half having a conversation. The TV had fascinated Echo at first. He couldn't stop watching the colors and shapes, the way people appeared up close, then far away, and then completely disappeared off the edge. He had tried checking around the back to see where they went, but he couldn't ever find them. How it all worked was a mystery.

Still, he had eventually grown bored with the TV. Flashing images could only provide so much entertainment. Annie still seemed interested, but Harley had stopped paying attention even before Echo had. They opted instead for resting their head on Annie's chest, only opening their eyes occasionally.

"Okay!" Annie gestured at the screen. "How does she still not realize her dad is in on it? She literally found a device to aerosolize the virus in one of his warehouses!"

Harley didn't even look up. "Lots of people have flawed thinking when it comes to their families. They excuse things they shouldn't."

"Yeah, I guess so," said Annie. "But that much? I mean look, she's giving him an out!"

Harley opened their eyes and glanced at the TV. "Maybe she's in on it too."

"No!" said Annie. "She's the main character!"

"Plot twiiiist," Harley teased.

Harley spotted Echo watching and propped themself up. "Hey buddy, wanna come sit on the couch with us?"

Echo looked away, embarrassed.

"It's okay Echo, come up here!" Annie patted a spot on her lap. Echo got to his feet.

"Come here! That's it buddy, there you go!"

Harley let out a gentle "oomph" when Echo slipped and jammed a paw into their stomach. He froze, worried that he had angered them, but they reassured him with a pat and a smile. Relieved, he created a space between the two humans and settled down into it. The whole process took a bit of digging, but it was worth it. *The humans were warm. And their scents were comforting.*

Echo hadn't been able to pick up the humans' scents in the lab—too much cleaning solution all over the place—but he had memorized them once they got home. Annie's hair still smelled of the rose petals in her shampoo, plus the garlic from dinner. Beneath that, her skin gave off a cool, gentle version of the odor all humans shared.

Harley's scent was quite different. Their short hair didn't hold the scent of shampoo like Annie's did, but traces of minty soap still clung to their skin. And their skin itself had a much stronger scent than Annie's. There was more oil and salt to it, and it produced a brand new scent whenever it mingled with the smells from Annie's skin. That was the smell Echo found most comforting. Annie and Harley together.

Harley lifted their head and gave Annie a gentle kiss. "Thank you for saving him."

"You saved him, too."

"Yeah. You know what I mean, though. You put so much work into it."

Harley laid their head back down on Annie's chest, ear close to her heart. "You have such a big heart. I've always loved that about you."

Harley smiled during that last part, and Echo realized it was the first time he'd ever seen them smile. He'd seen a smirk, sure, or a small tug at the corners of their lips, but never a *real* smile. He *loved* their smile.

"You always get so lovey when you're sleepy," Annie teased.

She ran hand through Harley's messy hair, and the smile grew. They didn't respond with anything other than a small, "Mhm," but that seemed to be all that was necessary. Harley closed their eyes again, sighing from time to time while Annie played with their hair.

Echo closed his eyes too. These were gentle people, and he felt safe. *Really* safe. Not just safe for the time being. Not just safe until the next morning, or until Jansson's footsteps echoed down the hall.

He couldn't remember feeling truly safe since the day he'd been taken from his mother at the breeding facility. And even then, the danger had been there. He had just been too naïve to see it coming. But squeezed between Harley and

Annie, Echo felt protected. Maybe even enough to go to sleep. Sleeping was a risky state, but something told Echo it would be alright. Besides, Ollie had been sleeping all night. He *surely* wouldn't do that if it was dangerous.

Echo didn't wake up until much later, when Annie and Harley left to head upstairs for bed. He stood, wobbled on the squishy surface of the couch, and then shook himself before padding after the humans. He stopped at the bottom of the stairs, but the humans kept going until Annie rounded the landing and spotted him.

"Do you want to come up with us, buddy? You're welcome to. Aspen and the bunnies sleep in their own little pens, but you might have to share the rest of the room with Vera."

Echo stared at Annie for a moment and then sat. It wasn't that he didn't want to follow the humans, or even that he was afraid of stairs. He *had* climbed them that morning, after all. Still, something about the stairs bothered him, so he just gazed up at Annie until she shrugged.

"Okay. Door's open if you decide you want to come up! Good night, buddy."

"Night Echo!" Harley called. Then the humans finished climbing the stairs and disappeared into the bedroom.

Echo kept staring at the spot his humans had disappeared for several moments after they were gone. *Good night, Harley. Good night, Annie.*

After a time, he padded back to the living room. The humans had turned out the lights, but moonbeams streaming through the window showed that Ollie hadn't wasted any time in claiming the couch. He managed to take up an excessive amount of space, but even a dog his size couldn't take the *whole* thing. There was still a little spot left at the end, and Echo promptly claimed it as his. *This would do,* he thought. *It was much better than a cage, after all.*

He curled up next to Ollie's outstretched legs and closed his eyes. The sounds of the house were disquieting at first, but one by one, Echo learned to accept them. The flushing of a toilet upstairs. Muffled bits of conversation from the bedroom, which grew infrequent and then disappeared entirely. Ollie's wheezing snores. The clatter of the ice machine completing its latest pieces of work.

After every little sound, Echo reminded himself that he was safe. That there was no need to worry. *The humans promised. This place is safe. Safe. Safe.*

Safe. He held onto the thought, almost as if he could take it between his jaws and keep it there forever. The thought of finally being safe was the most peaceful idea Echo had ever encountered, and he hung onto it until long after he fell asleep.

Chapter 11

Annie and Harley were gone on Echo's fifth day at home. They'd been gone most of the previous day too, because it was a "Monday." Annie said that meant she and Harley had to go to work, and the same rule applied to Tuesdays.

Harley always left for work at a much more reasonable time than Annie, but they also got home later. It was a routine Echo supposed he'd have to get used to. That was alright. It was much better than the routine at the lab, and the long weekend with the humans had done wonders in helping him adjust.

The humans had been occupied with something called a press release on Saturday, and most of Sunday was spent on countless phone calls about Annie's video. Echo hadn't realized a video could make the phone ring so much, but he didn't mind. Phone calls always left the humans with at least one hand free for scratches. As for the content of the calls, Echo didn't understand much except that Flatiron Life Labs had claimed the videos were either "doctored" or "fake." That part hurt. He'd *been* there. Felt the acid pouring into his lungs. None of it *felt* fake.

After Annie and Harley had arrived home on Monday night, Echo managed to learn quite a bit from their conversations. Annie worked as a field manager for a solar company. Echo wasn't sure what that meant, but he gathered that she spent a lot of time standing on top of houses and carrying heavy things. That was part of what made her so tired every day, but a good portion of it also came from the mental exhaustion of being a "queer woman in charge of a whole team of men." Echo didn't fully understand the implications of that statement either. He was proud of Annie for being in charge though, even if it wore her out.

Harley worked at a university in a nearby city called Denver. Their job was in the university's queer resource center, and that morning they had a very important meeting advising university officials on better accommodating trans students. Echo didn't know exactly what that meant, but Harley seemed pleased with the outcome of the meeting, so he was happy for them.

Harley also advised the student animal rights group on campus. Echo didn't know much about the group, besides that Sophia was a member and that they met on Tuesdays, which meant Harley would be home later than normal. The humans had explained that Annie would be home on time though, so there was no need to worry. Echo wondered if that meant he could expect her any time soon. He certainly hoped so, but he wasn't very good at keeping track of time.

Echo shook himself and jumped down from the couch, eliciting a series of protests from Aspen. The little chicken had actually become somewhat cuddly during the short time he'd known her. She kept her distance while Echo was up, but when he napped, he'd often wake to find her nestled against his stomach. *She's not so scary,* he thought. He'd actually started to enjoy their naps together.

Where did Ollie go? Echo wondered. The big dog had been on the couch when he went to sleep, but had disappeared.

He knew Bear and Moose must be upstairs—that was where they stayed when the humans were gone—and Vera was curled up in a sunspot on the desk. Vera was friendly enough, but she preferred napping over playing, and Echo had already napped enough for the day. It was time to play, and he needed Ollie for that. He took one last look around to make sure he hadn't missed anything, and then set off to find his friend.

Playing with Ollie had been quite intimidating at first. Echo had actually run away the first few times the big dog jumped at him, but he eventually learned what was going on. He took to following Ollie just about everywhere after that. It led to plenty of playtime, of course, but it also had another purpose. Ollie knew when to eat, or when to go outside, or when the humans were in the right mood to drop food under the table. The only place it *wasn't* a good idea to follow Ollie was the grass. Echo wasn't ready to risk that.

Ollie wasn't in the kitchen, but Echo was forced to stop his search there when a strange figure floated by the window above the sink. Strange figures were *not* supposed to simply float by windows. *Something wasn't right.*

Echo raced to the back door for a better look. A man with a hood pulled low over his face strode across the backyard, hands shoved deep in his pockets. From time to time, he would creep over to the side of the house to look at something. He moved with a skittishness that suggested he wasn't experienced in trespassing, but that didn't give Echo much comfort. He couldn't see the man's face. Without that, there was no telling who he was or what he wanted.

The man disappeared from view, and Echo nearly panicked. *Where were the other windows? He had to keep watch over the house!*

He rushed toward the stairs to cut the man off. There were no windows on the stairs though, and none in the closet either. That left the window at the end of the laundry room, but what if he had already passed that one? *What if he was doing something dangerous at that very moment and Echo couldn't see it?*

Echo raced into the laundry room, claws skittering against the hard floor. The window was high, but he could see through it if he stood back far enough, and it didn't take long to spot the man. *He was there. Just outside the window.* He seemed to be looking at something below the window, but the hood obscured so much of his face that it was hard to tell. *What could he be looking at? The ground?*

The man cleared his throat, and the sound floated into the laundry room through the dryer vent. *The dryer vent!* Echo had listened to the chirping of birds through that vent every morning since Saturday. It was the only path between the laundry room and the backyard, so the man *had* to be looking at that. The thought made Echo's hair stand on end. *The intruder wanted to come inside.*

Through the dryer vent, though? Humans couldn't possibly squeeze into such small spaces, could they?

Echo was still pondering the question when Ollie plodded into the laundry room behind him. The big dog spotted the intruder almost immediately. A low growl rose in his throat, and he pushed Echo aside as he advanced toward the window. A deep, angry bark suddenly exploded from his lungs, so loud that Echo jumped. Two more barks followed the first one, but it still took the man several moments to spot the dogs.

Do what Ollie does, Echo told himself. *Ollie knows what to do.*

With all the courage he could muster, Echo marched up behind Ollie and let out the loudest bark he could. It came out as nothing more than a forceful wheeze that pained his throat, but Ollie was loud enough that Echo didn't think anyone noticed.

The man fled toward the fence. The dogs gave chase, Ollie barking and Echo wide-eyed and wheezing. They reached the window just in time to see the man duck into a sleek black car parked by the curb. Echo was only barely tall enough to see through the window, so the car disappeared from sight almost as soon as it started driving away. Ollie kept barking furiously though, and he didn't stop until the sound of the car's engine was only a faint whisper in the distance.

Echo panted at Ollie, who promptly turned and marched toward the kitchen. The big dog had scared the intruder off, but that only served to make Echo more worried. Ollie *always* knew what to do, and his reaction confirmed that an intruder's presence in the backyard was *not* normal. It was something dangerous, something to be afraid of. It was something for the humans to handle, but Echo had no idea how to communicate such a complex concept in terms the humans would understand. Annie and Harley were smart, but even *they* couldn't ward off a threat they didn't know about. And that made Echo nervous. *Was this place really as safe as he thought?*

Chapter 12

Echo spent most of the next day on the lookout for the intruder, but his fears slipped away when Harley returned home early. He followed them around all afternoon, but they seemed too busy to offer him more than a few pats or the occasional kiss. Somehow, that made Echo even more excited to see them. *Harley was preparing something. Something big.*

A string of lights on the back porch...a candle on the table...something delicious cooking on the stove...and something even *more* delicious in the oven. Echo hoped he would get a taste of whatever it was, but even that seemed less important than finding out what Harley was up to. There was something in the air. Not just the smells. A feeling. *What could it be, though?*

It wasn't until Annie's key turned in the door that Echo got his answer. Harley was there in a heartbeat, greeting Annie with a long kiss.

"Happy anniversary," they said when they finally pulled away.

Annie ran a hand through her hair in the way she only did while talking to Harley. "Thank you. But...what is all this?

I thought we agreed we weren't doing anything big this year because we couldn't afford it, and everything's still so busy..."

Harley grinned sheepishly. "I know. That's why we're doing it at home. And I kinda just went along with the busy part so I could surprise you. Come on, you really think I wouldn't make time for you?"

Annie blushed—something Echo had never seen her do before. "I didn't do anything for you though...I'm sorry."

"That's okay," Harley said. "Food's outside. The weather's nice, so I thought we could eat on the porch."

"Okay," Annie gestured at her greasy jeans. "I'm pretty gross from being on the roof all day. Is it okay if I go shower and change into something nicer?"

Harley nodded, and Annie stood on her tiptoes to give them another kiss. "I'll be quick!"

Echo continued helping Harley while Annie was gone. *He'd been right! A special surprise for Annie! How exciting!*

After everything was done, Harley sat at the porch table to wait. The beginnings of a song drifted out of a portable speaker they'd set up earlier, but it was quickly cut off and replaced by a new one. Annie came down only halfway through the second song, dressed in a skirt and sweater. Her hair was still messy and wet, but she ran a hand through it anyway as Harley pulled out a chair.

"Breakfast for dinner," they announced. "I know you were saying the other day that you hadn't had pancakes in a long time."

"Thank you," Annie smiled. She turned her gaze toward the ground. "You're so good."

Harley and Annie sat at the table for a long time, talking more often than eating. Ollie and Aspen eventually joined Echo on the porch, and to the humans' credit, they did offer the dogs a few pieces of pancake. Aspen was apparently not allowed to have pancakes, but she seemed satisfied with the slice of banana Harley gave her.

Annie was about to bite into her last bit of food when a new song made her set it down. She stood up, grabbing Harley's hand and pulling them onto the grass.

"You know the rule about this song," Annie grinned.

It wasn't exactly graceful, but Echo's humans looked so...*beautiful* dancing under the string of lights in the yard. Harley's dark eyes drank in every detail of Annie's face, and Echo didn't think he'd ever seen Annie have so much energy after a day at work. *They were wonderful together.* Annie twirled as the beat picked up, and each of the humans began softly singing along.

"...Cause I, I, I—"

"—never want to—"

"—Wake, wake up without you..."

A hooded figure peering over the fence caught Echo's eye, but he was so enamored with his humans that it took several heartbeats to register the danger. He bristled and leaped to his feet, squinting at the spot he'd seen the intruder. But there was no one there. *He was gone. Or perhaps he'd never been there at all.*

Annie twirled again, snapping Echo's attention back to the humans. *There's nothing to worry about,* he thought. *The only humans here are dancing.*

"…and I'm not scared of the dark anymore—"

"—not as long as I'm with you…"

And the dancing was beautiful. The humans were so happy, so lost in each other and the music. Echo wanted to dance someday. Not with music—music didn't matter much to him—but with his humans. He wanted to feel so lost and free that he couldn't help but dance. To let his paws move all on their own and take the rest of his body with them. Not yet, though. He wasn't ready, and he was okay with that. For the time being, it would be enough just to watch.

Chapter 13

A whole day gone by without any threats from the intruder. Perhaps Ollie had scared him off for good. Or perhaps Echo had simply imagined him staring over the fence the night before. Maybe he had been worried for no reason, and the human had just been curious. *Humans got curious and sniffed around new places too, right?*

Either way, Annie and Harley were home for the night again, which comforted Echo. They had gone to bed a long time ago, but Echo hadn't been able to sleep. Instead, he sat with Vera on the desk, staring out the window. Flashes of light bounced off each other in the distant darkness, a display that was both beautiful and terrifying. *Something big was happening out there.*

The sound of rain on the roof had been pleasant at first, but Echo found the flashes and distant rumbles that followed troubling. *Whatever was out there was getting closer. What kind of creature—or thing—could possibly cause that much noise? And what if it wasn't friendly?*

Echo glanced at Vera for what must have been the tenth time. He kept waiting for her to turn and flee or give some other indication that it was time to take shelter, but she hardly reacted. All she did was stare out into the night, watching with an almost infuriating patience. Echo couldn't smell a single trace of fear on her. And Ollie was even less concerned. *He* was sound asleep on the couch, apparently uninterested in whatever was heading toward the house.

The house is not the lab, Echo told himself. Different things happened there, and windows certainly weren't a luxury he had experienced in his cage. He supposed it was possible that Vera and Ollie had seen this type of event before, and that their reactions were a perfect model for how he should behave. The older animals *did* have seemingly endless knowledge about how things worked. Still, Echo couldn't stop his heart from racing after every rumble. *What if he was the only one who realized danger was on its way? Wasn't that a possibility too?* After all, whatever was out there was definitely getting closer. And louder. The intensity of the rain had increased to an almost violent level, and he hadn't just *heard* that last rumble. He'd felt it in his chest.

Suddenly, the sky split open. A blinding flash of light crackled above the house, accompanied almost instantly by an explosion that left Echo's ears ringing. He felt his bladder emptying all over the desk, and he briefly worried about how disappointed the humans would be. He couldn't make it stop though. Maybe it didn't even matter. *The sky was falling. Everything was ending, and they were all going to die.*

Echo forced a glance at Vera and saw that she was also paralyzed by fear. A second glance revealed that something more was wrong, though. She wasn't *just* afraid. Her entire body had gone stiff, even as she fought to move back from the window. Echo was powerless to do anything but watch as the cat swayed and toppled off the desk.

Ollie was there only a heartbeat after Vera hit the ground, sniffing at her rigid body. Echo stared, utterly terrified. He *wanted* to jump down, wanted to help Ollie with Vera, but all he could do was stand in his little puddle and watch.

It got her, he thought. *Something out there got Vera.*

She started moving then, but it was somehow even worse than when she had been frozen. Her head went first, rotating up and to the side while the rest of her body remained stiff. Then her legs began to quiver as if some muscles wanted to kick out, but others wanted to relax, and others wanted to hold a rigid position. Vera's mouth opened slowly, painfully, like there was some unseen force prying her jaws apart against her will.

Ollie gave the cat one final sniff and then bolted toward the stairs, barking so loudly that the neighbors might have heard. His feet pounded out an irregular beat on the steps, only matched in volume by his voice. And even through that, Echo still couldn't force himself to move. He couldn't stop staring at poor Vera, her face contorted in a silent scream, her neck twisting until that screaming face was forced down into the carpet.

Annie's groggy voice floated out from the bedroom.

"I got him. Go back to sleep."

Still barking, Ollie clambered down the stairs. He paused over Vera for a moment, sniffed, and then raced back to Annie. He did this at least three more times, barking the whole way.

96 | A R I S   A U S T I N

Vera finally stopped convulsing and went limp on the floor, almost like she was sleeping. *But how could she be sleeping after all that?*

Echo swallowed hard. *What if she was dead?*

Annie finally stumbled around the corner, pulled along by a frantic Ollie.

"Ollie, calm down," she said. "Ollie. *Ollie!* Shh. Listen, calm down. I know it was loud, but it's just thunder. You haven't been afraid of thunder for years, buddy."

Vera's eyes opened to narrow slits, and she struggled to stand. She was barely strong enough to pull her face from the carpet, but that was enough. *She was alive.* Echo breathed several sighs of relief.

Annie was so focused on Ollie, she didn't even see Vera until Ollie finally ran to the disoriented cat. An audible gasp came from Annie's throat then, and she rushed to Vera's side.

"Oh, I'm so sorry, baby. Did you have a seizure? I'm sorry."

Annie jogged to the kitchen, flicking on lights as she went. She returned a moment later with two small pills and sat, propping Vera's head up with her leg. All traces of drowsiness had disappeared from her voice, replaced with a mix of genuine concern and stern command.

"It's okay, sweetie. It's over now, you're okay. Come on, swallow. Swallow, baby girl. Good girl."

Vera lifted a paw in an attempt to prevent Annie from massaging the second pill down her throat, but she was too weak to do anything more than rest her pad against Annie's wrist.

"I know baby, I know you don't like it. I promise I'm not trying to hurt you. It's just your emergency meds."

Vera gagged as the pill went down, but then she relaxed and allowed Annie to pet her. She squinted up at the ceiling, panting and confused. Several moments later, a weak *mew* escaped her mouth and she managed to lift her head on her own.

Another rumble of thunder shook the house. It was quieter than the previous one, but it startled Echo enough to make him realize he was still standing by the window. He scrambled to get down, but slipped in the puddle of pee and fell into it with a wet *slap*. Too frightened to be embarrassed, he immediately picked himself up and bounced from the chair down to the floor.

"Oh, Echo," said Annie.

Echo slinked under the desk, trying to avoid Annie's gaze. *Look at this mess,* he thought. *She's going to be so mad.*

Annie wasn't mad, though. At least, she didn't give any visible indication that she was. Instead, she stood slowly, taking care to ensure that Vera's head wouldn't fall again. Then she disappeared into the kitchen and returned with a roll of paper towels and a spray bottle.

"It's okay buddy," Annie said as she closed the blinds above the desk. "It's just a thunderstorm. They happen sometimes. We'll keep the blinds shut so it isn't so scary, okay buddy?"

She knelt and reached under the desk with a soapy paper towel, gently wiping the pee from Echo's fur.

"It's okay buddy," she said again. "Accidents happen, especially when you're new to potty training."

She patted his damp fur and frowned. "We might have to give you a bath tomorrow, but it's not a punishment, I promise. It's just to get you nice and clean again."

Once Echo was clean—or, clean enough for the time being—Annie stood and set to work wiping up the mess on the desk. "Good thing Harley left their laptop in the kitchen instead of on the desk tonight, huh? Although I guess that would have been pretty funny."

When she finished, she bunched up the paper towels and headed back to the kitchen. "Let me wash my hands and then I'll come back to make sure everyone's alright, okay?"

Another rumble of thunder sounded just as she returned from the kitchen. Echo flinched, and Annie gave him a reassuring smile. "You're really scared, aren't you buddy? Do you want to come back upstairs with me?"

Echo didn't move. He just glanced from Annie to Vera and back, trying to process everything that had happened.

"No? Well, maybe I'll just stay down here with you, then. It might be good to keep an eye on Vera, anyway."

Annie crossed the room and flicked off the light, then stopped to scratch Ollie's neck on her way back.

"Thank you for coming to get me," she said. "You're such a good big brother to all of them. You're a good boy, Ollie."

Annie scooped up Vera and settled down on the couch, then cradled the cat in one arm while she spent several moments using the other to prop herself up with pillows. When she was finally done, she patted her lap.

"Up here, Echo! Come on, it's okay! I'll keep you safe from the thunder."

Echo jumped onto the couch and circled the area before settling down on Annie's lap. He waited for Ollie to hop up too, but the big dog simply stretched out in his spot on the floor again. *How did Ollie manage to stay so calm?* Echo wished he was brave enough to sleep on the floor, but he felt much safer on Annie's lap. *It's safe with Annie,* he thought. *She promised.*

Vera, exhausted from the seizure, fell asleep almost instantly. Echo expected Annie to go to sleep too, but she spoke up after only a few moments. She whispered so she wouldn't wake Harley, but Echo could still hear just fine. His hearing was much better than Harley's, anyway.

"It's okay to be afraid, Echo. Sometimes scary things happen, and it's perfectly normal to react to them. Everyone is afraid of *something.*"

She rested a hand on his back, and the scent of rose petals wafted down from her hair. Echo *loved* that smell. It comforted him.

"I get scared sometimes too, you know. It's easy to play it off like I don't. Easy to act tough. People ask if I'm afraid of going back to jail, and I tell them no. I know it's a possibility, and I'm prepared for that. It doesn't really scare me if it's for something important.

"Because of that, people assume I'm brave, and I just kinda roll with it. It's easy for me to say I'm only afraid of failing you guys, but I'm scared of a lot more than that. I'm scared of spiders. I get scared of monsters from movies, and being alone in the dark. I get scared that even in a supposedly safe city, someday some creep in a bathroom is going to take an issue with Harley's existence and I'll lose them.

"I get scared when people yell. Especially men. And I'm *terrified* of getting hurt. I got caught inside a lab last year by a security guard who wasn't supposed to be there. He started yelling, and then he started coming at me, and I was *so scared* he was going to hit me, Echo. I had to climb out a second-story window to get away. Not because I was afraid of being caught—I mean I was a little—but mostly because I didn't want him to hurt me. Something popped in my knee when I hit the ground, and it still hurts from time to time. That's why I have a limp some days. Kind of ironic, huh? I got myself hurt because I was afraid of getting hurt.

"Sorry, I'm blabbing again and I don't even know where I'm going with it. I guess I just want you to know that being afraid is okay."

She was quiet for a moment, and it almost seemed like she was done. Echo could smell the tension on her breath, though. *She still needed to get something off her chest.*

"And I dream," Annie said. "I dream about everyone I left behind on every single rescue. There's nothing like hearing ten thousand voices all trapped in the same shed, all calling to you at once, and knowing there's only room in your arms to carry a few. I dream about those voices even when I can't remember their faces anymore."

Annie fell silent for a longer time then, and the darkened room was quiet except for the drumming of the rain and the now-distant roll of thunder. Echo flinched whenever the thunder got too loud, but he managed to stay calm. *Annie gets scared too,* he thought. *It's okay.*

"Sitting in the dark like this reminds me of Shadow," Annie said quietly. "I guess I haven't told you about Shadow, huh? Do you want to hear about him? I know it's late, but I'm not tired if you aren't."

Echo didn't respond, but he listened intently for whatever Annie planned to say next.

"Shadow was so special to me," she said. "He's a big part of the reason I do what I do today. He was already old when we met, but I bet he still had a few good years left. I was pretty new to the shelter—I'd only been there a few months—but I'd never seen anyone as depressed as he was when he first got there. His family just left him there after loving him almost his whole life."

Annie shifted her legs, prompting a sleepy Vera to stand and readjust herself.

"Good girl!" said Annie. "You're feeling a little better, huh? There you go, go back to sleep. There you go, sweetie.

"Anyway," she said. "I spent a lot of time with him to try and help him get better. And he did! It was amazing how much energy and personality he had once he finally got back to being himself again.

"I don't know if he ever knew, but it wasn't just a one-sided kind of thing. It was later on, but he really helped me out of a bad situation. I was with this guy, and he seemed really great, but in hindsight I think he was actually just good at making it look that way. Some bad stuff happened one night, and on impulse, I went to see Shadow afterward. I probably would have gone right back to the guy if it wasn't for Shadow.

I was way too forgiving and trusting when I was younger, and I guess manipulative people could smell that or something. I just wanna see the best in people, you know? But something Shadow did that night—maybe it was the way he listened so well, or the way he actually *growled* when I mentioned the possibility of going back—kept me accountable.

"I know it seems weird that I felt such a need to be honest with a dog I didn't live with about a guy he'd never met, but I promised Shadow I would do the right thing for myself. And I just couldn't break that promise. He was so trusting of everyone, kinda like me. Kinda like you. I wasn't going to be another person who let him down. Not after his family betrayed him the way they did."

Annie sighed, and Echo detected hint of pain on her breath. "I guess I did let him down in the end, though. I know it wasn't really my fault. It wasn't really even the shelter's fault. We were just doing the best we could in a broken system. And…maybe I should have stayed in that broken system and tried to fix it from the inside. It felt like the whole world was broken though, and I just didn't know what I could possibly do. I think I realize now that working within the rules does a lot of good, but it isn't always enough to un-break the world. I don't know if that makes sense. I still don't have an answer, really. But what good are rules if someone gets hurt because of them?"

Annie sighed again. "I loved that dog, though. I only knew him for a year, but I loved him so much. I think he knew that in the end. And I think he loved me, too. He made me want to do better. I didn't want to just stand by feeling so powerless while someone who deserved to live died.

"I didn't know what that meant for a long time. I didn't want to feel powerless, but I didn't know what that meant or how to make it happen.

"That spring—about five months after Shadow died—we had a company picnic fundraiser type of thing. By then, I'd gotten pretty good at making myself get tougher. We'd only lost one more dog, but he was sick, and I was careful not to get attached to him or anyone else. It didn't hurt so much, but I also didn't feel like *me*. If we're being honest, Shadow's death burned me out. My heart hadn't been in the work for a while, even though I wanted it to be, but I didn't get the final push to leave until that picnic.

"Anyway, it was towards the end of the picnic. I'd been sitting with my coworker Deb, but she had gone to the bathroom. And I was looking at the half-eaten burger on her plate, and something about it snapped me out of the daze I'd been in. I started thinking about how awful it was that everyone around me was eating animals at a fundraiser meant to *save* animals. I'd known the disconnect was there all along, but it bothered me so much more than usual that day."

The idea baffled Echo. He could never imagine eating someone like Vera, or Bear or Moose or Aspen.

"I don't know why it got to me so much in that moment. And at the same time, I don't know why it took so long to get to me. I couldn't understand how we could possibly ever change the world if people could be so callous.

"So I decided I had to stop being callous. I decided not to let the awful things I saw turn me into a hard person. I got up and left the picnic because I didn't want to cry in front of everyone. And when I got home, I sat in my car all by myself and cried for the first time since Shadow died. I thought about a lot of things while I was crying. I thought that I could do better. That I could do more. But most of all, I thought that I wanted a change. I didn't want to feel numb anymore, even if that meant leaving my job at the shelter. I knew it was one of the best shelters in the state, but…I just couldn't do it anymore. Any of it."

Echo wondered if Annie still cried. She seemed much too tough for that, but she had also promised not to let the world make her hard. *Did she need to cry right now?* He couldn't smell any signs of it, but he decided he would be there for her if she did.

"I took the job at the solar company only a few weeks later, which meant moving out here. I always told myself I'd go someplace without a winter, but I was pretty desperate. My checks from the shelter didn't last very long, and I was pretty close to not being able to make rent. It was just the first job I got an offer for, and I took it. I think maybe it was meant to happen, though. I never would have met Harley if I hadn't moved here. And only a few weeks after I got here, I met some people who taught me how to run rescues. We saved three little lambs who were supposed to end up as someone's Easter dinner, if they even made it that far. They were all pretty sick. Tuberculosis. I guess it happens on a lot of feedlots."

Echo had no idea what kind of creatures lambs were, but he decided that if they were little, they were probably closest to either the bunnies or Aspen. Annie continued with the story before he could think much further than that.

"Anyway, we named them Barry, Bertie, and Bentley. They had to spend a long time in quarantine at the vet, but they were so happy when they finally got to go outside. I never would have done something like taking lambs from a feedlot a few months earlier, but I had decided I was done following the rules when the rules hurt someone. And in the moment they first stepped outside, I knew I had done the right thing. I mean, here were these lambs who by all means should have been dead. But instead, they were enjoying the sun, growing up with each other, playing…it meant so much to them to be alive. I knew I wanted to do that for more animals, and I didn't feel powerless anymore.

"Maybe I should have felt a little powerless—it's a big fight. That's probably why it was a fight I stayed out of for so long. It's hard, knowing there are so many animals you can't save. But being able to walk in and rescue even a few was so powerful. I could get to know who they were and see them experience things they never would have if they'd gone to the slaughterhouse. *That* was what I'd been looking for when I took a job at the shelter. It was what I'd been looking for when I was a little girl making picture books about saving animals.

"I helped with two more rescues after that, each one only a few months apart. There were the three hens, Maggie, Artie, and Pigeon. And Amina, a little calf from a dairy. I had to take a break when Cam—he was Ollie's adopted big brother—got cancer. And then I met Harley and we were really busy building a life together, but I never forgot about rescuing. When I finally got back into it, I felt like there were already a lot of hands on deck for farms. That's why I started running rescues in labs.

"I do regret leaving the shelter sometimes. I want to be able to feel like I'm helping animals with my day job again, not just in my free time. Maybe I'll work at one again someday, but I was just so burnt out when I left. I wasn't exactly thinking this many years into the future."

She sighed. "Anyway, I don't know if it makes you feel any better, but I think you and your siblings are getting more justice than most of the others. It's probably because you're dogs instead of mice or rabbits, but maybe it's also that people are starting to wake up a little bit. Only that one newspaper took the story at first, but after we released our footage and linked Oasis to the tests they were doing on you, a lot more outlets picked it up. People are pissed. There's even a boycott of Oasis gaining momentum.

"A lot of the people boycotting are probably just buying other products that were tested on animals, but hopefully a few of them did their research and switched to brands that don't test. And maybe all the noise about it will make other brands rethink their testing policies. I guess I just want you to know that the people who hurt you are getting some kind of consequence, buddy."

Annie suddenly sat up, startling Echo. "Oh, I forgot the best part! I hid my phone in the lab you know, and we got footage of that businessman watching the experiments and not shutting it down. We included it in the video release, but we didn't realize how significant it was until a newspaper identified him as Spencer McMachen—founder and CEO of Oasis. That clip of him telling the researchers to keep pushing you is *not* sitting well with people."

Echo whined. He remembered exactly who Mr. McMachen was. He remembered the man's stare. The way he forced Ross and Jansson to make it even *worse*. And how just before meeting Mr. McMachen, he had seen those dead mice filled with pins and needles. He shuddered.

Annie smoothed out the hair on Echo's back. "I'm sorry, bud. You probably don't like thinking about that place. I won't be so specific. But this has a good ending, I promise. Oasis probably could have convinced the DA to press plenty of charges against us, but they already have their hands so full of bad press, I don't think they want to damage their reputation even more with a court battle. Instead, it looks like McMachen is being forced to take the fall for the company. He actually stepped down from his position on Monday night.

"I'm sure lots more than him knew about the testing, but at least there's some justice there. Spencer McMachen, forced out of the company he built. And so fast, too. We only released the video on Saturday. At least *he* got what he deserved.

"The lab doesn't seem to be affected much, but they haven't repeated their claim that the video was fake. Maybe that means they won't press charges. I'm sure there's something they could get us on, but they're probably trying to stay out of the public view while Oasis takes all the heat. I guess we'll see in the coming months.

There are still a lot more who need rescuing from that place. I think I gathered from room labels that there's a whole bunch of bunnies like Bear and Moose on the second floor. I hate the idea of leaving them behind, but maybe someday, when they get complacent about security again. And unfortunately, there are still plenty of other labs to visit…"

Echo wasn't sure exactly when he fell asleep. It must happened at some point though, because the next thing he remembered was Annie trying to get up without waking him. The gray light of dawn glowed against the blinds, and Annie grinned sheepishly.

"Sorry, buddy. I didn't mean to wake you. I'm running a little late already, though."

Echo shook himself and jumped off the couch. He didn't mind. He could always go back to sleep, and probably would later on.

Vera had disappeared while he was asleep, but he didn't put too much effort into finding her. It wasn't all that unusual that she'd slipped away during the night. She liked sleeping in small, hidden spaces, and had probably curled up in the closet or laundry room. Annie wasn't worried, so Echo decided he didn't need to worry either.

He followed Annie to the laundry room, where she slipped into a wrinkled pair of jeans and a faded hoodie that had the symbols "SolArt" written over an image of a yellow sun. She smiled at Echo, put a finger to her lips, and led him to the backyard so he could pee. He still didn't like the grass, but Annie and Harley seemed happier hosing off the concrete than cleaning stains out of the carpet.

"I'll be back later, okay buddy?" Annie yawned. "Hopefully a little early. I could use a nap.

"Tomorrow's Saturday, so Harley and I will both be home all day. Oh, and on Sunday, Sophia's going to bring Jakey over and you two can have a playdate! Would you like that?"

Echo followed Annie back inside and over to the front door. He waited while she grabbed her keys off the key hook, and bent down to kiss the back of his neck. Annie *always* remembered not to touch his face. He loved that about her.

"See ya' later, okay bud?"

Annie slipped out the front door, but Echo stayed and listened for several moments after she disappeared. He listened to the deadbolt sliding into its place in the doorframe. Listened to the jingle of Annie's keys as she made her way to her car. He listened to the engine start and then fade in the distance.

When the sound was finally gone, he returned to the couch. Harley wouldn't be up for a while still, and he figured he might as well take a nap while he waited for them.

Chapter 14

"Harleyyy...Helloooo...Earth to Harley!"

Annie waved a hand in front of Harley's face, which got them to finally glance up from their phone.

"Hm?"

"Sophia's going to be here soon. Do you want to maybe change out of your pajamas?"

Harley had already gone to the trouble of changing out of their pajamas once that morning, when they had gone to church with Annie. The pajamas were back on as soon as they got home again, though.

"Oh yeah, sorry." Harley took a distracted sip of coffee. "Have you seen McMachen—the former CEO of Oasis—have you seen his Twitter?"

"...No," Annie leaned over Harley's shoulder. "Wow. Do you think he could really do that? Get a law passed to put a life sentence on open rescue?"

"Mandatory minimums are slowly falling out of favor, so it seems like most lawmakers would find it excessive," said Harley. "And even if they didn't, the courts would. I'd hope he doesn't have much political clout after his little scandal anyway. But, money talks. *Especially* to our Senator Long. And to hear McMachen tell it, he and Long go way back."

"Mm. Well, hopefully nothing comes from it. He seems like kind of a big talker. Why are you following his Twitter anyway?"

Harley shrugged. "I like to keep an eye out for anything that might come our way. I keep tabs on lots of peoples' social media."

Annie pulled Harley out of their chair. "Well, enough Twitter rants. Go get dressed."

She gave them a quick kiss, then smirked and added, "Coffee Breath."

Annie picked up Harley's phone while they climbed the stairs. "Sounds kinda like a conspiracy theorist. Listen to this, buddy. "These so-called activists are really corporate terrorists. Maybe sponsored by China or Russia to destabilize the economy. Regardless, my livelihood is ruined and prosecutors are too lazy to pursue. If they won't take action, I will!"

"We really got to him with that video. I guess he should have thought about the consequences before he tortured you though, huh?"

Echo stared blankly at Annie. Most of what she said had gone over his head, but he guessed Mr. McMachen was still in trouble for being bad. That was good, at least.

He heard Sophia and Jakey coming a heartbeat before they knocked. It took Annie ages to get the door open, but the wait was worth it. *Jakey!* Echo and his brother walked around and around each other, sniffing and snorting and greeting. *Jakey had so many new smells! Leaves, and shampoo, and a dusty carpet, and happiness!* That was the most important part. Jakey was happy. Echo could *smell* how much he adored Sophia. *This was good. This was very good.* Echo stared up at Annie, smiling and wagging his tail.

Annie smiled back. "Are you two happy to see each other?"

Echo didn't have time to react to the question before Ollie nearly bowled him over. He greeted Jakey with the same energy he had when he met Echo, sniffing and pawing and panting until Jakey looked more than a little overwhelmed. Annie eventually had to pull Ollie away.

"Dude, calm down! You're gonna scare him!"

She turned to Jakey. "This is Ollie. Don't worry, you don't have to be afraid of him. He's just excited to meet you, I promise."

Echo gave his brother a comforting look to confirm the information. *Don't worry. Ollie is safe. Annie wouldn't let him near us if he wasn't.*

Annie and Sophia talked while they waited for Harley to return—how school was, how work was, how the animals were doing—Echo didn't listen too closely. He was just excited to be back with one of his siblings. And to see that sibling *thriving!* The wound on his paw had nearly healed, and his coat was so full and bright, Echo wondered if Sophia bathed him every day. *That sounded terrible.* Jakey seemed happy though, so maybe he didn't mind all the baths.

Harley came downstairs wearing jeans and a black t-shirt. They gave Sophia a quick hug before leading the way to the back door, opening it, and gingerly stepping out of the way so Ollie wouldn't bowl them over. Jakey had joined Ollie in the yard in a matter of heartbeats. They scared a couple of birds up into the trees, but stopped to wait for the rest of the group after the initial excitement had faded. Ollie barked impatiently.

"Okay! We're coming!" Annie called as she, Sophia, and Harley strolled into the yard.

Echo happily followed behind them, but pulled to a sudden halt just before stepping off the porch. *He had almost stepped into the grass. He had to be more careful.*

But what was the problem with going into the grass? Ollie and Jakey were okay, and so were the humans. How could it possibly be the same as needles? Echo sniffed warily at the stray blades creeping onto the porch. *They didn't smell like needles.*

"Echo!" Annie called out. He glanced up to see her across the yard, patting her legs and motioning him over.

"It's okay, buddy! Look, it's safe!"

She patted the grass with a bare hand. When that failed to convince Echo, Annie dropped to her knees and rolled onto her back.

"Look buddy! It's totally safe—" a sputtering laugh cut her off as Jakey came over to sniff her face. Once she recovered, she stood again and walked to the porch.

"I know you're scared, buddy. But it's really okay. I wouldn't ever let anything bad happen to you. You know that, right?"

Echo gave her a nervous yawn.

Sophia appeared at Annie's side, followed by Harley only a moment later.

"What's wrong?" Sophia asked.

"He's scared of grass for some reason," said Harley. They put an arm around Annie's waist. "You two go play with Ollie and Jakey. I'll hang out here with Echo."

They turned to Echo. "Come on, buddy! Let's go sit down!"

Echo padded after Harley and took a seat next to them on the porch steps. It wasn't that he didn't like being outside. He *loved* being outside. It was what he'd wanted for most of his life. The days were getting warmer, and the sun felt wonderful on his back. He couldn't get Dr. Ross out of his head, though. Dr. Ross and the needles. And the mice. And needles sticking out of their little bodies at every angle, just like grass.

"It's beautiful, isn't it buddy?"

The question snapped Echo back to reality. Harley was staring out into the yard, where Annie and Sophia were running from Ollie and Jakey. Or chasing Ollie and Jakey. It seemed to switch every few steps, which was how the game was always played. There were a lot of smiles though, and a lot of mock screams followed by laughter. Jakey's tongue lolled out of his mouth as he nearly caught Sophia, then narrowly avoided crashing into Ollie.

"The way they can just let go," Harley went on. "It's a gift. Or a skill, maybe. I don't know. Some people have it though, and it's beautiful."

Harley smiled one of their rare smiles. "Especially Annie. I love that about her. So many of us build up these hard, tough shells to protect ourselves, and some of that hardness inevitably seeps inside. Not Annie, though. She keeps the world from turning her hard, somehow. I always thought that was so special about her. I wish I could do it."

Sophia and Annie stopped for a breather, apparently relieved that Jakey and Ollie had become occupied with chasing each other. That arrangement only lasted a few moments though, and the humans were back in the game long before they caught their breath.

Echo sighed. *It looked like fun.* He laid himself down on the warm concrete and nudged Harley for a little attention. They scratched him absently, lost in thought but still careful to avoid touching his face.

"You know how we met?" Harley asked. "My flight had just gotten in at the airport and I was waiting by the baggage claim. There was a big group of refugees—mostly families—coming in on a flight just after mine because they'd made it through all the screenings and been approved for resettlement. They don't usually all come in on one flight like that, but it must have happened somehow.

"That was back in the big mess of a run-up to the 2016 elections, so accepting Syrian refugees was a pretty contentious topic. Somehow, the information about their flight got out, and there was a nasty little group of protesters waiting by the escalator. There weren't *too* many of them, but they had some awful signs. "Go somewhere else." "Keep our country safe—Keep Islam out!" You get the idea."

Echo wasn't entirely sure he got the idea, other than the fact that Harley didn't like the people with signs. He decided to keep listening for more clues.

Harley sighed. "I rolled my eyes and figured I should just ignore them. After watching for a few more minutes though, I decided I would confront them. Most of the refugees *were* going somewhere else. I haven't actually been to Lebanon since I was little, but I still have a few relatives there, and we talk from time to time. Neighboring countries like Lebanon were way past full, and these people needed a place to go. I mean, they were fleeing for their *lives*. Some of them probably watched their children and siblings die, but these assholes had the nerve to accuse them of being terrorists."

They clenched a fist, then quickly relaxed it. "I'm all worked up about it now, so you can imagine how pissed I was then. If Annie built her shell out of happiness, I must have built mine out of anger. It's a reflex, I guess.

"I probably wasn't that far off from getting into a fistfight, which I'm not proud of. But then Annie came dancing out of this tiny group of counter-protesters with a boombox. That's a type of big speaker that plays music. People don't use them much anymore because they're so huge.

"Anyway, Annie came dancing out with this boombox on her shoulder, blasting the Red Hot Chili Peppers so loud no one could hear anything else. And she was just *laughing*. Every time someone yelled something at her, she turned it up. And then the refugees started coming up the escalator, and instead of a bunch of assholes yelling at them, they see Annie dancing totally out of control to "Around the World". A couple of the little refugee kids thought it was so fun, they even started dancing with her. I can honestly say I've never seen anything else like it.

"I *had* to talk to her. I *may* have…pretended to lose my bag so I could get into the same train car as her for the ride home. But she picked a seat next to me, not the other way around! When I asked, she just gave me this cute little smirk.

Said she wanted to make sure those people had a dance party waiting for them when they got to their new home."

Out in the yard, Annie pretended to trip. She lay motionless for several moments until Ollie went to investigate. As soon as he sniffed at her cheek though, she jumped up with a mock scream and danced away. Ollie barked and gave chase.

"Somehow, she made her shell out of the soft stuff most of us are trying to protect. And she gets hurt. I know she does, even if she doesn't want me to see it. But she stays *her* instead of getting all tough and hard like so many people do. Like I do. I've spent so much time in my shell, I can't even decide when it comes off anymore. I kinda hate that about myself sometimes."

Echo thought he understood. It was *scary* to be soft. Being soft made it easier for the needles to get you. But growing hard took something away. Echo trusted—even loved—Annie and Harley, but he couldn't just do it by default. He had to *choose* to trust. *Choose* to be vulnerable, to flop on his back for belly rubs or sleep out in the open. And even though he could still do all those things, it took work. He was tired of having to work to be happy. He wanted to build his shell out of softness, just like Annie. He wanted to dance. *Was it too late for that?*

Harley patted Echo's back. "No one's gonna blame you for being tough and hard if that's what you need though, buddy. After everything you've been through…it's okay if you need to be scared, or defensive, or happy, or whatever you want. We'll love you no matter what."

They glanced down at their phone, which had a full screen of human symbols too small for Echo to pick out. There were only three large enough to see, positioned at the very top of the screen: M-o-m.

Harley turned it off before Echo had the chance to think much about what M-o-m was. *Definitely something serious,* he thought. He could smell it in Harley's breath.

"We'll love you no matter what," they repeated. "Trust me, bud. I know about needing to build a hard exterior to get by."

Chapter 15

Echo opened an eye to see what the disturbance was. *Just Moose joining the nap. Nothing to get worried about.*
Moose had established a pattern of cuddling up to Echo's belly on rainy days. Echo hadn't thought of the bunnies as being particularly cuddly at first, but it turned out Moose was when he got cold enough. He had to share the space with Aspen of course, but he didn't seem to mind.

Echo didn't mind either. In fact, he liked it. Naps with Aspen had become the new normal, and Moose only made things better. He was soft and gentle, and his breathing was comforting despite its rapid pace. Combined with the patter of rain on the roof, Moose's rhythmic breaths made Echo sleepier than almost anything else. He'd already managed to nap half the day away, even though it was Saturday and the humans were home.

No, Harley isn't home, he thought. *Just Annie.* He could remember Harley leaving that morning. They had gone to get coffee with their mother, which was very important because they hadn't seen her since high school. That was when Harley had "come out," which apparently made their parents angry enough to kick them out of the house. Then after nine years without talking, Harley's mom had texted them out of the blue. She was even driving all the way up from Harley's hometown. Annie said that was a good sign, and even said she was looking forward to finally meeting Harley's parents once things were settled. Harley, on the other hand, hadn't said much at all. They'd been floating between hope and despair for several days, and Echo was glad it was finally time to get it over with.

He wondered what Harley's mom looked like. He hardly remembered what *his* mom looked like, but he knew she'd been big and warm. And she fed him with milk. She smelled like dry food and unwashed fur. He spent long mornings curled up next to her belly, just like Moose and Aspen. Those first days with his mother had seemed so safe. *So warm.* Echo had hardly even wondered why they were in a cage. The memories of those distant days filled his heart, and he drifted off to sleep still thinking of his mother and siblings. He could almost smell them…

Echo dreamed that the hooded man was back again. Back by the side of the house, just outside the laundry room. He had seen him through the window, had tried to bark out a warning to his humans. Muted coughs were all that came out though, and no one in the house heard him.

The hooded man heard, though. Echo locked eyes with him only a moment later, and a chill ran down his spine. *He knew those eyes. He knew that face.*

Calm and emotionless as ever, Dr. Ross drew back his hood. He put a finger to his lips, then held up a fistful of needles. Echo wanted to run, but he was paralyzed. *Why couldn't he stop watching?*

Dr. Ross's hand passed through the window like it was nothing more than water. His fingers closed around Echo's throat, gingerly lifting him off the floor and pulling him through the glass. It was only then that Echo regained control of his body, and he lashed out with a fury he didn't know he had. *No more needles,* he thought, and bit down on the man's wrist with all his strength. When Dr. Ross didn't drop him, he bit down again. And again. But Dr. Ross didn't even flinch. And when Echo finally looked at his wrist, it seemed completely untouched. A second chill ran down his spine.

Dr. Ross set his handful of needles down on the windowsill, selected one, and spent several heartbeats carefully examining the point. Then he whispered, "Just a blood sample today, Echo. That's all we need."

He pushed the needle into the usual spot on Echo's forelimb. But then instead of drawing blood, he picked up another needle and pushed it into Echo's back. And then another in his leg. And his ear, and his back again, over and over until he looked like the poor mice from the cart. Every single stab hurt worse than the one before it, but Dr. Ross didn't stop. He just kept going, needle after needle after *needle* until there was only one left.

Dr. Ross turned the last needle over in his hand, and Echo braced himself for the point's bite. It never came, though.

"Well, I suppose we can't use them all today," Dr. Ross whispered. "We want to have something for next time."

Then he tucked the needle into his coat and dropped Echo in the grass. He left without a second glance, and Echo was powerless to do anything but watch him disappear into the red haze that had formed across his eyes.

Less than a heartbeat later, Annie and Harley's voices echoed through the backyard. Ollie's, too. *They were looking for him,* he thought. *He was going to be okay!*

Something was wrong, though. Annie passed within a few steps of him, but she didn't even notice him lying there. And Harley did the same a moment later, calling out for him the whole time. *Why didn't they see him?*

It was only after the humans disappeared back around the corner of the house that a terrifying realization dawned on Echo. *They couldn't see him because of the needles. There were too many needles sticking out of him, and all the humans saw were blades of grass.*

Echo tried to call out, tried to let them know where he was, but his severed vocal cords were too quiet for the humans to hear. And he was getting weaker. So weak, he wasn't even loud enough to be heard by Ollie. And somewhere out there, Harley was crying. Crying and crying…

Echo woke with a start and shook the dream away. *He was in the living room. The needles were gone. He was safe.*

Harley was still crying though. They were seated on the couch, leaning against a distraught Annie.

"It's okay," Annie said. "I've got you. Big, deep breaths. Come on. Breathe with me. Do you want to tell me what happened? Big, deep breaths, sweetie."

Echo stared, caught between wanting to comfort Harley and the need to comfort *himself* after the dream. *So many needles.* He shivered, and it was only then that he noticed Moose and Aspen had both moved across the room. He hoped he hadn't kicked them while dreaming.

Harley lifted their head and managed to get out a few words between gasps. "I. Let myself think. Things would be different."

"Breathe," said Annie. "Big, deep breaths. We can wait a few more minutes to talk if you need to."

Harley let out a shaky breath. "I thought my mom reaching out—I thought it meant she was starting to adjust. Starting to accept me."

They sniffed and fought back a fresh wave of tears. "Things were okay for the first half hour. Really awkward, but okay. She asked if I was good with just coffee, or if I wanted to get some sausage or bacon off the menu. I explained that I don't eat animals anymore, and she seemed to accept it. I asked about dad, and she asked where I was working and if I liked it. There were some awkward silences, but that's the most we've talked since I was a kid.

"And then she put her coffee down and said, "I miss you." That was it, I thought. She was finally going to apologize for everything. I told her I missed her too."

Harley took a deep breath. "Then she nodded and said, "So please, give up all this…this *transgender stuff* so we can be a family again."

"I stared at her for at least a minute. Waiting for her to say something else. Waiting for her to realize she was still being hurtful. And then I realized she already knew that. She still doesn't want *me*. She wants the kid she thought I was.

"So I just got up and told her I didn't have to take this from her. And then I drove home. And I thought I was fine. I didn't cry at all on the drive, but then... sorry."

Harley's face contorted in pain, and tears began to roll down their cheeks again. Everything was quiet for a while. The only sounds were Harley's soft sobs and the whisper of Annie's fingers combing through their hair.

Then Harley's eyes regained their razor-sharp focus. Their voice took on a sudden edge.

"As if *I'm* the reason we haven't talked in years. Not the way she rejected me. Not the look on my dad's face when I told them. Not the way I spent my last two weeks of high school sleeping on my English teacher's couch. Not the way they didn't come to see me graduate from college, or watch us get married."

The muscles in Harley's jaw tensed. "They didn't come to our *fucking wedding*, Annie!"

Annie opened her mouth to say something, then closed it again. Harley stood.

"They act like I can just turn off who I am. I *can't. I can't. I can't!*"

Their voice rose with every "I can't" until they were practically screaming. Echo stared, wide-eyed. *Harley was never like this.*

"Do they *know* how long I tried to do that? Do they *know* how long I hated myself for not being able to? I wanted to *die,* and I didn't stop wanting to die until I realized that *maybe* it would be okay to love myself! That maybe they were wrong. That I wasn't going to Hell for just being me. That maybe, *just maybe,* it was *okay* to be me. I'm *not* going to go back to that. I'm *not going* to go back to wanting to die! Fuck that, and fuck *them* for trying to pull me back in!"

No one said anything for a long time. Harley just stared, looking almost as shocked at their outburst as Annie. The scents of anger, sorrow, and pain were so strong that Echo couldn't even tell which human each one was coming from.

When Harley broke the silence, their voice was so small it was hard to believe they'd been yelling only a few moments before.

"No matter how old I get, it still hurts."

They collapsed back onto the couch, and Annie's arms were around them in a heartbeat. She held them while they cried, hugged them so tight they could barely move.

After a few moments, Vera jumped onto the couch and curled up in Harley's lap. She kneaded their legs and purred, staring up at them expectantly until they patted her head.

"Hi baby," they whispered.

Harley wiped their eyes and looked at Annie. "Sorry. I haven't gotten that worked up about them in years. Or anything else, really."

"It's okay," Annie said. "It's safe to let go around me. You know that, right?"

Harley nodded and sniffed.

What Vera had done worked so well, Echo decided he ought to help. He padded to the couch and gently climbed up, one paw at a time. Then he settled down on the only empty cushion and rested his head by Harley's hand.

A stray tear fell from Harley's face and landed on the back of their wrist. Instinctively, Echo licked it up, and kept licking until Harley's whole wrist was warm and wet. It was something his mother had once done. *It made him feel safe.*

Annie's hand inexplicably flew to her mouth, and when Echo looked up, he could see tears forming in her eyes. Then she reached down to pet him.

"Good boy," she said.

Harley moved to pat Echo's back. Then they rested their head on Annie's shoulder and closed their eyes before letting out a long, shaky breath.

Chapter 16

"…So after all of that, they asked if I could just get a hold of the architect myself. He argued a little at first, but he eventually agreed to modify the plans and put at least one gender-neutral bathroom in the building."

"They made *you* call him?" Annie asked.

"Yep," Harley sighed. "Even though it was supposed to be in the plans in the first place. How was your day?"

"Well, it was slow. We were starting a new commercial install, but something got mixed up and our delivery truck showed up with residential size panels. And I guess I was out of it, because I didn't even notice until we had a few of them on the roof already. So then I had to call in and explain that the order was wrong, and we had to take everything down. Then we had to wait for the right size to come, which took almost three hours. We all still got paid for the time we were sitting around, but I think some of the guys were pissed because it's going to take us an extra day to finish this job now."

"I'm sorry," said Harley. "Sounds like we both had rough days."

"Yeah," said Annie.

Echo lifted his head in anticipation as Annie picked up a piece of roasted potato. He loved roasted potatoes, mainly for the grease and salt all over them. He had positioned himself under Annie's chair for dinner that night, because she was normally more prone to dropping things. Unfortunately, the potato made it all the way to her mouth without any trouble.

He wondered if Ollie was having any luck over by Harley. Or how Vera was faring up on top of the table. *Probably not as well as she could be.* Ever since he first saw her sitting up there, Echo hadn't been able to understand the way she wasted the opportunity. If *he* could be up on the table, he'd have cleaned off both Annie and Harley's plates before they even picked up a fork. Sure, the humans might get angry, but they never stayed angry for long.

Echo loved his humans. He loved his new home, which felt more real every day. The nightmares were slowly disappearing, as were his fears about the hooded man. He hadn't peed in the house since the thunderstorm, and although grass still made him nervous, he'd been brave enough to walk to the edge of the porch and sniff it two times that day. Maybe someday, he'd even be willing to touch it.

The days since Harley's meeting with their mother had been calm, and Annie had begun taking Echo on longer walks with Ollie. *That* was one of the best parts about home. Real walks. *Outside.* Sometimes for so long his legs got tired. They were so much better than the brief loop around the hall at Flatiron Life Labs.

Annie put another potato in her mouth, then started talking long before she finished chewing.

"Oh, I meant to tell you! It's been around a month since we got Echo and his siblings out. I think I'm going to start looking for a new target soon. Do you have any ideas?"

Harley raised their eyebrows. "Is that going to be too soon? You don't want to get too much attention from prosecutors. And…you need time to take care of yourself too, Annie."

"Yeah, I know," Annie said. "I think it'll be okay though. I'll just look in another county. The time we spent investigating Flatiron was much shorter than normal, because we had a tip on it. But even then, it was a few weeks before I was ready to go inside. And it'll probably be a few months before I find another place to go into. Till then, it's just research."

"Okay," said Harley.

There was an awkward silence. Then Annie said, "Thank you for looking out for me."

"You're welcome."

Echo watched Annie scoop the last bit of food off her plate and into her mouth. *Nothing dropped tonight. What a disappointment.*

"Have you heard anything else about McMachen?" Annie asked, changing the subject.

Echo bristled at the name.

"No," said Harley. "He's been pretty quiet. At least, he's been quiet online. Who knows what he's saying behind closed doors, but I doubt he has much credibility anymore."

"Hopefully," Annie nodded. "Powerful men seem to suffer far fewer consequences than the rest of us, though."

"Especially the rich, white ones," Harley added.

Annie nodded and pushed out her chair. She collected Harley's plate and her own and, to Echo's delight, placed them on the ground.

"I'm exhausted," she announced. "I know it's early, but do you want to go cuddle for a while and then go to bed early tonight? I'll take care of those before I leave for work in the morning." She gestured to the plates.

"I'll get them," said Harley. They kissed Annie's cheek and gave her a gentle push in the direction of the stairs. "You go get ready for bed. I'll be up soon."

Harley stood over Echo while he and Ollie finished licking the plates, but he hardly noticed their presence. Traces of barbecue sauce and baked beans demanded his immediate attention, and Harley would still be there when he was done.

He glanced up at Harley once he finished, smiling and licking at the corners of his mouth. Harley seemed tough, but he'd learned that they were just as willing to give him treats as Annie was, if he was persistent enough.

Harley bent down to pick up the plate and scratched Echo's head. "You just got food. I watched you, remember?"

Echo licked Harley's face, and they patted his back.

"Maybe next time," they said.

Unfazed, Echo flopped down to the floor and rolled on his back for a belly rub. Belly rubs were one of the first things he'd discovered from watching Ollie, and they were *wonderful*. Harley obliged for a few brief moments, but the belly rub ended only shortly after Ollie finished licking his plate.

Harley washed and dried the plates, then paused before climbing the stairs.

"Anyone coming up? Vera?"

Vera didn't move from her spot on the table. Ollie was already on his way to the couch, and Echo always slept downstairs. He liked it better that way.

"Alright," Harley said. "Sleep well, babies. I love you."

Harley flicked off the light and climbed the stairs. Echo waited until he heard them safely arrive in the bedroom, then padded down the hall to see if Ollie had left any space for him on the couch. *Good night Harley,* he thought. *See you in the morning for breakfast.*

Chapter 17

Echo had trouble falling asleep that night. He normally went to bed right after the humans did, but they'd gone upstairs so early that he wasn't tired. It probably didn't help that he'd napped most of the afternoon. After what felt like half the night, he gave up on sleeping and jumped down from the couch. *Ollie hadn't been giving him much space, anyway.* He shook himself and padded to the kitchen to see what Vera was up to, but she was missing from her spot on the table.

Probably sleeping in one of her little hiding places, Echo decided.

It took quite a bit of effort to determine that she wasn't curled up in the kitchen sink, which had been Echo's first guess. It wasn't until he finally jumped high enough to peer over the edge of the counter that he remembered Vera only slept in the sink during warm afternoons. *Of course she wasn't in there.* But that *did* give Echo a clue. She'd probably made herself a nest of towels in the closet by the laundry room. It only took him a heartbeat to pad over to the closet door and hear her gentle snoring. *There she was.*

Echo didn't feel the need to wake Vera—that would probably make her grumpy—but tracking her down had provided at least a little entertainment. Hide and seek was a game he often played when he was bored, though it was usually just "seek," since no one else knew they were playing. He'd wander from room to room, just to see who he could find. It provided much more of a challenge in the daytime, when he didn't actually know where most of them were. With five of the family members upstairs and Ollie asleep on the couch though, Vera was the only one who needed finding.

He padded back to the kitchen and stared outside for a while. It was peaceful night. A slight breeze rustled the leaves on the bushes, but the rest of the world had gone to sleep with the sun. Echo loved it. Being able to look out the window whenever he wanted was something he would *never* take for granted. He never could have wandered to the window in the lab. If he was unable to sleep there, he simply had to wait in his cage.

Echo's ears registered the sound of an engine. Engine sounds by themselves weren't all that abnormal, even in the night. Humans drove places at all kinds of strange times. But he recognized this particular engine, and it made him nervous. He raced to the front window, arriving only a heartbeat before the sleek black car came to a stop by the curb. A hooded figure climbed out, and the fur along Echo's spine stood straight up.

The hooded man circled to the trunk and removed a large container. It was heavy, judging by the way he carried it, but he walked quickly anyway. Echo watched the man until he disappeared from view. He started to follow him toward the laundry room, but paused before he got there. *What if it really was Dr. Ross, back to poke more needles into him?* He knew he should wake Ollie, but Ollie was still on the couch, and

Echo wasn't about to risk losing track of the intruder. *If only he could bark!*

Echo cautiously crept into the laundry room, keeping to the shadows so he wouldn't be seen. He arrived at the window just in time to see the hooded man set the container on the ground and leave again. *What was he up to this time?*

The sound of liquid sloshing inside the container floated through the dryer vent, but Echo had no way of determining what it was. There was no use trying to sniff at it; the vent was between the dryer and the wall, and there was no way Echo could reach back there. The only things he could smell from his spot by the window were lint and the litter box.

The hooded man returned with a newspaper, which he pulled apart as quietly as possible. Then he knelt down, disappearing from sight, and sounds became Echo's only clues as to what he was doing.

He was pouring the liquid out. The newspaper caught most of it, but a few occasional splashes fell to the ground. Then the wet newspaper—no, not completely wet—the part in the man's hand was still dry. Echo could tell from the way it rustled between his fingers. Wet or not, it was stuffed into the dryer vent, and then the process was repeated with another piece.

Each time a new wad of paper was stuffed into the dryer vent, it got a little harder to hear what was going on. But a smell replaced the sounds, and it was *strong.* So harsh that it made Echo wrinkle up his nose. *This could not be good. He needed to do something.*

The man stood, coming back into view with the container. He dumped the container's remaining contents on the wall around the dryer vent, sloshing it back and forth until it was almost entirely empty.

Echo made his decision.

With all the strength his legs could muster, he launched himself toward the window, jumping just high enough for his claws to clatter against the glass. *He couldn't bark,* he thought, *but he might still be able to frighten the intruder off.*

The man raised his head with terrifying similarity to what he'd done in Echo's dream. Echo shrank back, worried about being filled with needles, but then the man's face came into view. *It wasn't Dr. Ross.*

Echo let out the loudest wheeze he could manage, and the hair on his back stood up even higher. His eyes met Mr. McMachen's for only a moment, but it was enough to make his blood run cold.

Mr. McMachen reached into his pocket and produced a small pack of matches. He struck one and used it to light the rest, staring at the flames for a moment as if purposely avoiding Echo's gaze.

Then he tossed the matches against the side of the house and ran.

Chapter 18

Echo backpedaled as the side of the house burst into flames. It was only a few heartbeats before the fire made its way inside, tearing through the gas-soaked newspaper and creeping up the drywall. The heatwave that washed over the laundry room stung Echo's eyes and burned in his throat.

Ollie suddenly appeared by Echo's side, barking at the flames. It wasn't an angry bark, or even a bark meant to wake the humans. There was fear in Ollie's voice. And that terrified Echo. *Ollie was never afraid.*

Echo and Ollie had retreated into the hallway by the time Harley finally came rushing downstairs. A bleary-eyed Annie stumbled down close behind in an oversized sweatshirt. Both of their eyes went wide when they saw the laundry room. Crackling flames had consumed the dryer and most of the wall. Thick black smoke poured through the door, dancing across the ceiling until it finally found its way to the smoke alarm. The resulting ringing only added to the chaos.

Annie began to choke, but quickly straightened. She took exactly four steps *toward* the flames, yanked the bathroom sink on, and soaked her sleeve in water. She pressed it over her mouth and nose before turning back to Harley.

"Bunnies," she said in a muffled voice, pointing at the stairs. "Aspen."

Harley nodded and offered the flames one last glance before racing back upstairs.

With her free hand, Annie reached under the sink and pulled out a tiny fire extinguisher. Then she took a deep breath through her makeshift mask, pulled the pin, and loosed a jet of white smoke at the flames.

Echo stared in awe as his human stood silhouetted against the fire and smoke, fighting back with smoke of her own. He thought of the way she had frozen up during the escape from Flatiron Life Labs, but that was a far cry from the Annie standing in front of him now. *This* Annie was intense and in control. *This* Annie would let the fire eat her alive before she let it touch the rest of her family. Echo could see it in every movement, every step she took toward the flames. Annie would protect the rest of them to her dying breath, a thought Echo found comforting and horrifying all at once.

Slowly, the fire retreated. Annie advanced, gaining back several steps of the burnt laundry room before the extinguisher finally sputtered out. She stared at the empty canister for a moment, turning it over in her hands before shaking her head and dropping it. The flames crept forward again almost immediately, seemingly intent on making up the ground they had lost.

Annie edged backward, returning her wet sleeve to her face. Echo and Ollie retreated with her, cowering beneath her legs. The smoke threatened to choke Echo, but one glance at a barking Ollie told him it wasn't time to run yet. *Follow Ollie. Ollie knows what to do.*

As soon as Harley returned with Bear, Moose, and Aspen, Annie pointed toward the front of the house. Echo's family made their way to the living room, humans doubled over to avoid the smoke. Annie yanked the front door open as soon as she reached it. The group stumbled outside, but they hadn't gone more than a few steps before Harley turned to Annie, eyes wide.

"Where's Vera?" they rasped. "She should have come running as soon as we opened the door."

Annie dropped her sleeve and sucked in a few quick breaths of clean air. "I'll find her. Take care of everyone else."

She turned to the dogs. "Stay with Harley. *Be good.*"

Then she put her sleeve to her mouth and ducked back inside. Her muffled calls for Vera floated through the doorway, carried on billowing smoke. Ollie followed Harley toward the street, but Echo hesitated by the door. *He couldn't stay outside. He knew exactly where Vera was.*

The smoke inside the house was much thicker than it had been only moments earlier. Even as close to the ground as Echo was, it curled around his face and tried to pry its way inside his nose. He squinted through the haze, but he couldn't see Annie anywhere. Worse, the fire made it impossible to find her by scent or sound. *He would have to catch up later,* he thought. *Vera first.*

Flames had consumed the entire laundry room by the time Echo reached the closet. The floor was so hot, he had to shift his weight from paw to paw to keep from burning his pads. *How hot would it be in the closet? Could Vera really still be in there? Why wouldn't she have gotten herself to safety yet?* It didn't seem like there was anywhere else the cat could be, though.

Thick smoke threatened to choke Echo, but he knew better than to cough. The smoke wasn't going to go away, and coughing wouldn't help any more in a fire than it did in the lab. He *couldn't* let himself start coughing. If he started, he'd never be able to stop.

Echo forced himself to breathe as he scanned the closet for any sign of Vera. Even in the tiny space, it took him several moments to spot her lying in a heap next to the towels. She seemed disoriented. Confused. Struggling to lift her head, just like after her seizure during the thunderstorm.

The realization made Echo's heart sink. Something— the heat, the smoke, the fire alarm—must have set off a seizure, and Vera wasn't going to be able to walk any time soon. *Where was Annie?*

Echo set his jaw around Vera as gently as possible. She tried to protest as he pulled her from the closet, but she was still too weak to do anything more than let out a confused *mew.* Even without resistance, she was difficult to walk with. She was almost as big as Echo, and a stray paw or tail dragging against the floor threatened to trip him at any moment. With Annie nowhere in sight though, he didn't see any options other than to keep going.

The stinging tears in Echo's eyes made it even harder to see, but he managed to make his way toward what he thought was the kitchen. He had to fight to force images of the lab out of his mind. It was easy to know in theory that this was different from the lab, that he wasn't strapped into a harness and mask. But so many things were the same. The air was bad.

He couldn't see, he needed to vomit, and every half-cough nearly sent him into a panic. *Focus,* he thought. *Focus on breathing. In. Out. In. Out. In.*

Where could Annie possibly be? Breathing was getting harder with every moment, and Echo didn't know how much longer he could carry Vera. He wondered if he should just head for the door and come back for Annie later, but a distant cough stopped him. It was faint under the crackle and hiss of the fire, but the closer he got, the clearer it was.

Cough. "Vera…" Annie's voice, scratchy and hoarse. *Cough, cough.* "Vera. Please come out sweetie."

Echo's eyes were so filled with smoke and tears that he walked right into Annie's leg before he found her. She was crawling on her hands and knees, searching for Vera in the cabinets beneath the kitchen sink between coughing fits.

"Echo…?" she seemed confused. Then she saw Vera.

"Good boy," she whispered.

Annie took Vera, cradling her in one arm and using the other to crawl forward. Echo followed so closely that he kept bumping into her, but the smoke was too thick to risk backing off. If he lost her now, he would be stuck in a haze of smoke and tears forever. Annie knew the way outside, and he had to trust that she could still see it.

They might not have made it if not for the back door in the kitchen. Annie cried out as she touched the burning hot handle, but she somehow managed to hang on long enough to push the door open. They stumbled onto the back porch together, gasping and choking. Even the concrete outside was hot. It took Echo several moments to blink the smoke from his eyes, and Annie had already reached the edge of the porch by the time he could see again.

He paused before following her onto the grass. The thought of stepping on grass was still terrifying, but a single glance back told Echo he had to risk it. Smoke poured out of the doorway, and dancing flames glowed beneath the kitchen window. The concrete burned against Echo's paws, and it only got hotter with every heartbeat. *Grass was the only option.* Echo took a deep breath, and then forced himself out into the yard.

He'd been half-expecting pain, like a hundred needles stabbing his paws. The pain never came, though. *It was safe!* He caught up to Annie in a matter of moments, and together they stumbled through the back gate. Harley was waiting in the front yard with Ollie, Aspen, and the bunnies, holding back tears and half-shouting into a phone. They paused when they saw Annie, nearly melted with relief when she wrapped her arms around them. And then the entire family collapsed into a giant heap of limbs and wings and smoke and tears.

"I...I didn't know if you were okay," Harley sobbed. "I should have gone with you. I'm sorry. Are you okay? I love you. I'm so sorry."

All Annie could offer in return was to cough and pull Harley closer. Ollie took on the role of licking Vera from head to toe, rousing her despite her protests. Aspen cocked her head to the side and watched. The bunnies didn't budge, except to huddle closer together on Harley's lap.

Echo allowed himself to splay out on the ground while he struggled to catch his breath. *His eyes and lungs burned like acid. Just like in the lab.* He panted hard, doing his best to fight off the panic rising in his throat. The eerie light cast by the fire didn't help his nerves, so he slowly shut his eyes. *It's okay,* he told himself. *The fire is far away. The bad air is gone. Just focus on breathing. In. Out. In. Out.*

"This is m…m-my fault," Annie sobbed. "It h-has to be my fault. I finally pissed off someone dangerous. But I never thought they'd try to hurt our family. I'm so sorry. If—if you want out, I won't blame you for leaving, and I want you to know—"

Harley cut her off. "Quiet. I would never."

Somewhere in the distance, a siren began to howl.

Chapter 19

The chaos still hadn't been resolved by the time the sun came up.

A neighbor had taken Echo and his family in shortly after the fire trucks arrived. None of them had been able to sleep though, especially not Annie or Harley. The way the fire had affected them was the part that upset Echo the most. Their eyes were bloodshot and hollow, but they still stayed up all night to check on the animals. And when Harley heard about how Echo had saved Vera, they held onto him for so long he thought they'd never let go.

When the sun came up, neither human seemed capable of pulling their eyes from the smoldering remains of their home. The house wasn't completely gone, but it wasn't completely there either. The wall where the fire had started was caved in, and the laundry room was more ash than anything else. Dark soot stains marked the walls above every window, and much of what wasn't burnt had been flooded by fire hoses. None of the humans seemed to know if they'd be able to repair the damage or if the whole thing would have to be rebuilt. Either way, Echo was without a home again. That hurt. He trusted Annie and Harley to figure out where they were going to live, but he would miss the house. *He felt safe there.*

The night had been long and frightening, even after the firefighters arrived. Firetrucks were *loud*, and the people who climbed out of them looked more like monsters than humans. Echo, Annie, and Vera had been forced to wear oxygen masks, which terrified Echo. He'd tried to turn away, tried to escape, even considered biting if it would keep the mask away. He hadn't been able to calm down until Annie scooped him up and, talking through her own mask, promised it was clean air. That she would never *ever* let someone hurt him. She held him close to her chest, which would heave from time to time. Then in muffled sobs, she'd thank him again for saving Vera.

When it was finally time for the masks to come off, the paramedic taking care of them scolded Annie. Apparently, he was unhappy with the way she had gone back for Vera.

"Pets are important," he said. "But we don't want people dying in burning buildings because they went back for their pets. Pets can be replaced. You can't."

Even through the overwhelming scent of smoke on Annie's sweatshirt, Echo could smell the anger on her. She seemed too tired to do much more than smolder, though.

"You're wrong," she croaked. "My *furniture* is replaceable, not the animals. They have lives of their own, and they want to keep them just as badly as we want to keep ours."

Annie coughed and grimaced at the man. "Besides, I promised I'd keep them safe."

Echo turned his attention back to the present. He was seated on the neighbor's couch, where a police officer and fire scientist were interviewing Annie and Harley. They had discovered McMachen's container in the grass near the fence, and several indicators pointed to the fire being started with gasoline. The lab hadn't come back with fingerprints or any other solid evidence though, which meant they could expect a long, tiring arson investigation in the months ahead.

"Can you think of anyone who might want to do this to you? An ex, or a colleague, or maybe a recently fired employee?" The police officer was stocky and short, but he still towered over Echo.

Annie ran a hand through her disheveled hair and sighed. "I think it might be my faul—"

Harley interrupted her. "You can't know that, and you need to stop blaming yourself or you're not going to be okay." It hadn't taken long after the fire for their voice to return to its normal stern tone.

They eyed the police officer, not bothering to hide their discomfort. "I'm a trans person with brown skin. We're a queer couple, I work in a visible position in queer advocacy, and Annie works on shutting down research labs that torture animals. Take your pick, I guess."

The police officer nodded. "It's going to take a long time to examine all those angles."

He looked at the fire scientist, who sighed. "I'll have the lab check the details against any currently existing profiles. That way, we can at least start by ruling out a serial arsonist."

Echo felt a pang of frustration. *He knew exactly who had done it, but he couldn't communicate that to the humans in terms they'd understand.* He whined at Annie.

"I know, buddy," she said. She pulled him onto her lap. "You had a stressful night. It's okay though. We're all safe, and we have insurance that should help us rebuild."

She sounded more like she was trying to convince herself than Echo. After a brief pause though, she spoke in a much more genuine tone.

"And you're the reason Vera's going to be okay. You did a good job. You are such a good boy Echo, and everything is going to be okay. I promise."

Chapter 20

It took a long time, but Annie was right. Things seemed like they were going to be more or less okay.

Echo's family spent a week sleeping on the neighbor's couch, and then spent several months in a little one-bedroom apartment while the house was put back together. It had been a tight fit, but they made it work. And just in time to catch the end of summer, they were finally *home*. The key sounded different when Annie turned it in the lock, and the whole place smelled wrong. Beyond that, there was no couch or desk or kitchen table. But the humans assured Echo that this was *home*. And he believed them.

Parts were familiar. Two of the living room's walls were the same old walls they'd always been. And the top of the staircase still creaked when it was walked on, just like it was supposed to. The laundry room, closet, and kitchen had been completely replaced though, and every surface in the house had been scoured with something that made Echo wrinkle his nose.

A broad smile suddenly stretched across Annie's face, and she threw her arms around Harley. "We're home! We're home, everyone!"

She giggled and danced around in a half-circle, which prompted a bark from Echo. He didn't bark much, but Annie was so excited that it seemed appropriate.

He hadn't even been able to bark the last time they were home. Echo could hardly believe they'd been gone that long, but it was true. His very first sound had been in the apartment. They'd been living there for quite a while, and he had curled up on the couch with Harley while they ate breakfast one morning. When Harley got up, Echo jumped down to follow. He misjudged the distance, which squeezed some air out of his lungs. And with the air came *a sound.*

Echo had stared at Harley, who seemed just as shocked as he was. Then he tried to make the noise again. When that worked, he went for a full bark. And it *worked!* It wasn't a great bark—it was quiet and excessively squeaky— but he had a *voice* again. Harley had been so excited that they called Annie at work and made her stay on the phone until Echo could show off his new voice. They learned later that when vocal cords were cut instead of completely removed, there was a chance they could eventually heal.

Of course, the apartment hadn't been all good. The tight space made Vera so grumpy that she once clawed Moose in the face just for bumping into her. The poor bunny hadn't even seen her, but Harley still had to rush in and rescue him. And Annie and Harley were stressed beyond all reasoning during the time there, spending long nights hunched over credit card bills and bank statements.

The police were working on McMachen as a suspect, but he had covered his tracks well and there was never enough solid evidence to charge him. That seemed to bother the humans. Echo had heard them say more than once that they didn't feel safe with him out there. *And what if he found them again?*

Later, news came out that McMachen and his friend Senator Long were aggressively pushing a minimum sentence bill—two years for anyone involved in an open rescue. McMachen had managed to present himself as a victim, going on and on about how Annie's video had cost him his livelihood. He and Long claimed they wanted to protect small businesses, and that Echo's rescue was a theft that deserved punishment. And it was working. Annie and Harley argued about it frequently; how certain it seemed that it would pass, whether it was worth it to go to prison for two whole years. Or who would take care of the animals if they were both sentenced, and if they should try to rush another rescue before the bill became law.

There was always good to balance out the bad, though. Sophia and Jakey were over frequently, and Annie's parents flew out twice to help with moving in and out of the apartment. The tight space also allowed Echo to get to know his family better. By the time they left the apartment, *he* was usually the one to seek Aspen and Moose out for naps.

As for the humans, they seemed to take significant comfort in posters they sometimes saw on walks. The first one had been stapled to a telephone pole downtown—they usually walked Echo downtown, since he still preferred sidewalks over grass—and the humans had been so excited that Annie picked Echo up to show him. The poster was simple: a black-and-white image of Annie carrying Echo out of Flatiron Life Labs. Over the image were the words, "Support Animal Rescue—Defeat Senate Bill 3880." Annie read it to Echo twice before pointing to his picture and calling him famous.

Echo loved the relief his humans got from those little victories. It was comforting to know they had at least some support. The relief never stuck around for long, but the humans' worry seemed to fade as the months passed. Echo supposed they might never get McMachen for what he did, and he supposed he could accept that if the humans could. As Harley so often said, bad guys didn't always get what they deserved.

Vera sniffed at the house's new carpet and rubbed against Annie's leg. Annie reached down to pet her.

"I know, baby! We're back home again!"

She looked at Echo and Ollie. "Are you guys ready to have a backyard again?"

Echo raced to the back door with his big brother, then waited impatiently for the humans to catch up. *Humans certainly took their time whenever something exciting was about to happen.*

Harley smiled one of their rare smiles. "They're all so happy."

Annie rested a hand on the door handle. "I know. I love seeing them like this."

Echo let out an impatient snort as Annie turned to grab Harley's face and give them a frustratingly long kiss. *So close. He wished they would hurry up and open the door.*

"I think…" Annie closed her mouth again before finishing.

"You think what?"

Annie sighed. "I don't know if this is a good time for this. But anyway, Dr. Reyes—that professor from your university who's running for governor—her campaign contacted me last week. She said she wants to do better for animals, and that it'd be politically valuable to be one of the first to really take a stand. She wants me to work under her campaign manager and advise on animal issues. And...I think I want to do it. It'll pay less than SolArt though, and it's only until November unless she wins."

Harley's eyes lit up. "Annie that's incredible! You've been looking for a way to help animals in your day job again!"

"Yeah," said Annie. "But...I just don't know if it's something I can even do. I mean, I didn't finish college and now I'm supposed to join a team of lawyers and strategists?"

Harley reached around Annie's waist and pulled her close. "Just because they went to school for longer doesn't mean they know more about this than you. You'll do great. Just promise to be careful."

They smirked. "*You* in politics, though. That'll be an adjustment for you."

Annie rolled her eyes. Echo whined at the door, which *still* wasn't open.

"I know," Annie said. "But at the same time, all this stuff with McMachen and Senator Long has made me realize it's one of the best ways to fight back. I could help change policy for the whole state. Shelters, labs, ag...even rescuing. I'd hit a lot of walls, but I think I could do some good, right? I think I at least want to try. Echo could be dead right now, but he gets to live instead. And so many more deserve that.

Everyone deserves the chance to experience life outside of a cage."

The door *finally* opened a crack, and Echo squeezed outside with Ollie. The humans followed, taking their time as usual.

Ollie raced out into the yard, barking at a few birds and then marking his old territory along the fence. Echo meant to follow, but he still couldn't help but hesitate before stepping on the grass. He hadn't been on grass since the night of the fire. Even on walks, he always stuck to the pavement. *Now that they had a yard again though...*

He glanced back at Annie and Harley, who smiled and encouraged him to go on. *It's safe,* he told himself. *It wasn't sharp back then, and the humans promised that it's still safe now.*

Echo took a deep breath and placed a single paw in the grass. He hadn't been able to truly feel it the night of the fire— his only concern had been getting away. Now, it felt *wonderful.* The surface was warm in the sun, but a refreshing cool touched his pad as he pressed down.

He took another step, and then three more. *Cool and green and soft.* Echo closed his eyes, shifted his weight from paw to paw. Relished in the sensation of the grass giving way beneath his toes. His tail began to wag, and he felt the sudden urge to *jump.* To run and prance and play. So he did. He jumped in the soft, cool grass, and it only made him happier.

Echo *loved* the grass. He loved his life, and his family. Ollie and Harley and Annie and Vera and Aspen and Moose and Bear. He could even learn to love this new home, he thought.

Ollie rushed past, barking as he went. Echo opened his eyes just in time to see Annie and Harley chase after him, arms stretched wide. That was how the game was played, and Echo decided he'd had enough of playing indoors. It was time to play outside, where he could run and run until his legs couldn't carry him anymore.

As soon as the humans turned to flee from Ollie, Echo joined in the chase. Annie screamed and laughed as she nearly collided with him, then turned to chase him back the other way.

Echo hadn't ever run so fast in his life. Wind stroked the fur on his face, and the sun warmed his back. The grass beneath his paws pushed him forward, lifting him up as if it too wanted to see him run. And running was exactly what he did. Running back and forth with Ollie and his humans, laughing and barking and playing in the sun. Even when everyone else stopped to catch their breath, Echo kept going. He knew they were staring at him, but he didn't care.

Ollie flopped down in the grass to rest. Annie drew her arm around Harley's waist and pulled them close. All Harley could do was wear one of those rare smiles.

And Echo?

Echo danced.

There are plenty of real-life versions of Echo and his family in the world, just like there are countless real-life versions of Flatiron Life Labs and Oasis.

It's up to each of us to pick a side. Learn more about how to fight animal testing at arisaustinauthor.com/standupforecho.

Hey there! Thank you for reading *Echo*. If you enjoyed this book, please consider posting a short review on Amazon and telling a friend. Sharing an author's work is the best compliment you can give, and your time is very much appreciated! You can also find me on Facebook for updates on future work: facebook.com/arisfortheanimals

I also recommend taking a look at *Shadow*. Before there was Echo, there was Shadow. Learn about Annie's past and the story of the shelter dog she loved so much. Available on Amazon.

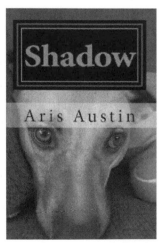

Hi, it's me! This is the part where I thank everyone who made this book possible and give those of you who are interested a little author bio.

I'd like to thank my partner Erica, who's always the first to hear my plans, my schemes, and my frustrations, and who is always willing to beta read ugly rough drafts. These books wouldn't be the same without all her advice and support.

I'd also like to thank Kevin from Beagle Freedom Project for his help on the behavior of dogs rescued from labs. I'd like to thank Kaelyn for beta reading, Ana for being my cover model, and Aidan for the pictures. I'd like to thank all the friends who support my work, and God, who I pray to for support just about every day of writing.

I'm an activist and author living in Colorado. I love spending time with friends of any species, and I'll never turn down a slice of vegan pizza. I'm on a mission to use books to make the world a better place for animals, and I'd love it if you'd join me! Please, if this book had an impact on you, take action. Check to make sure your cosmetics and household products aren't tested on animals (if they don't clearly indicate that they weren't tested on animals, you can assume they were—most of the biggest brands still use animal testing). If they were tested on animals, replace them with animal-friendly items. You can find information about brands that don't test on animals at arisaustinauthor.com/standupforecho.

Support open rescue. Challenge the idea that animals are our property, only put on this planet to be used in our experiments. And be sure to keep an eye out for future work from me. You can learn more on my website, arisaustinauthor.com, or on my Facebook page at facebook.com/arisfortheanimals. If you have questions for me, I'd love to hear them at arisaustinauthor.tumblr.com

See you around!

33046067R00099

Made in the USA
Middletown, DE
10 January 2019